The Right Way to Sing

LINDA M

D1495473

ALLWORTH PRESS
NEW YORK

Acknowledgments

I would like to thank my colleagues at the High School of Dundee for their comments and suggestions and the School of English at the University of St. Andrews for granting me a leave of absence to enable me to finish this book. Finally, I would like to thank Dr. Paul Sergeant, a willing student of Chapter 4, for his practical help in preparing the manuscript, and my editor, Jill Day, for her invaluable work on the text.

© 2005 Linda Marquart

09   08   07   06   05   5   4   3   2   1

Published by Allworth Press
An imprint of Allworth Communications, Inc.
10 East 23rd Street, New York, NY 10010

Cover design by Derek Bacchus
Page composition/typography by SR Desktop Services
Cover photography by Giorgio Palmisano

ISBN: 1-58115-407-0

Library of Congress Cataloging-in-Publication Data
    Marquart, Linda.
    The right way to sing / by Linda Marquart.
        p.   cm.
    Includes index.
    1. Singing—Instruction and study.   I. Title.

    MT820.M36   2005
    782.04'2—dc22

                                2004028828

Printed in Canada

This book was previously printed in Great Britain as part of the "Right Way Plus" series, published by Elliot Right Way Books.

Contents

Lea Salonga

Lea Salonga began her professional career at the age of seven in a production of *The King & I* in her native Philippines, but her biggest (and most life-changing) break was the role of Kim in the West End and Broadway productions of *Miss Saigon* for which she won the Laurence Olivier Award (London), Drama Desk, Outer Critics Circle, and Tony Award (New York). While in the New York production, she was tapped to record the singing voice of Jasmine in the Walt Disney animated classic *Aladdin*.

Shortly following her departure from *Miss Saigon*, she was offered the part of Eponine in *Les Misérables*, which she played on Broadway, in concert as part of the Dream Cast at the Royal Albert Hall in London, in the West End, and as part of the National Tour. She saw this role as a personal mission to prove that nontraditional casting does work.

As if playing one Disney heroine wasn't enough, she was overjoyed to be the singing role of Mulan in Disney's *Mulan* and in the straight-to-video sequel, *Mulan II*. She also gave voice to the role of Mother in Hayao Miyazaki's (*Spirited Away*) *My Neighbor Totoro* with Dakota and Elle Fanning, Timothy Daly, and Pat Carroll.

Her most recent appearance on Broadway was as Mei-Li in a reconceived production of Rodgers and Hammerstein's *Flower Drum Song*. She first played this role at the Mark Taper Forum in Los Angeles. Other theater credits include *Into The Woods* (The Witch), *My Fair Lady* (Eliza Doolittle), *They're Playing Our Song* (Sonia Walsk), *Proof* (Catherine), and *Baby* (Lizzie). She has performed in concerts all over the world, released many studio and concert CDs, and has sung for numerous heads of state. She currently resides in Los Angeles with her husband Rob.

Foreword

By Lea Salonga

When I was asked to write the foreword to Linda Marquart's *The Right Way to Sing*, of course I wanted to read her book first, in order to get a clear idea of what it was all about. Surely the title would say it all, and I was expecting a sort of "user's manual" of singing, if you will, something to give the novice vocalist something to get excited about. Well, my expectations were met . . . and more!

I only wish I had this book (or something just like it) when I was a young singer beginning my career.

At the onset of my journey, I was a young girl of seven, and knew nothing more than the joy of being able to produce a melody and the pleasure derived from it. Singing was, at the time, a hobby, and one that I knew I would keep while I was on my way to a medical career. However, when I was eighteen (and getting accustomed to the smell of formaldehyde), my path quickly changed. I auditioned for a brand new West End musical called *Miss Saigon*, and, thus, my medical career was derailed. I would no longer be a doctor, but instead, a working musical theatre actor. Sure, while growing up in my native Philippines I had done quite a few musicals and released a few records, but I never thought of music as a full-fledged lifetime career. The excitement of opening a West End musical was so great! I was sent off to London with well wishes, prayers, plenty of sweatshirts and hope for the best. *Miss Saigon's* run began auspiciously enough, and my voice held up in spite of a lack of vocal training. I was running on adrenalin, and unfortunately, my supply was beginning to run low. To summarize my story, three months into the run, I ran into severe vocal trouble, and it took a caring voice doctor, a good voice therapist, and an incredible singing teacher to nurse my young voice back to health, and give it a new strength that I never knew was possible. I returned to the show after three weeks of therapy and silence (for someone who enjoyed talking as much as singing, this was TORTURE!) with a voice that was stronger and better supported, physically. The rest of my run went like a dream. I realized then that a strong technical knowledge of singing would ultimately ensure the survival of my "instrument."

I have found this book to be, in spite of its compact size, a very thorough and extensive "nuts and bolts" manual that will benefit both the novice and the seasoned pro. It contains technical information on vocal classification as well as an extremely detailed description of the physiology of the singing voice (the mechanism of the singing machine, as it were). At the end, Linda lists other professional options and advice, and answers whatever questions a singer may have.

What you will not find in this book, or in any book for that matter, is the magic formula that will turn you into a world-class singer overnight. Barbra Streisand didn't sound that way when she popped out of the womb (although there are times I think she did). Singing takes a lot of practice and hard work . . . like learning how to swing a golf club, you learn one step at a time, training your muscles to respond to your every command. And boy, once you get the hang of it, it's so much fun. I've been singing for more than twenty-five years, and though my professional career is finite, the joy of singing will last a lifetime.

Whether you're planning to embark on a professional career, or just win points on karaoke night, this book is a great place to begin. Singing isn't meant just for the supremely gifted vocalist; it's also a great hobby to take up and a wonderful way to release tension and stress. For me, singing is both a living and a way of letting go of the worries of the world.

Chapter 1:

Introduction

Singing – there's no mystery about it

'Being able to drive a car is a gift of nature.'
  'I'll never be able to drive – it's just not in my genes!'
  'Drive a car? Either you can or you can't, and I can't!'
  'I love to drive up and down the road in front of my house, but I'd be too embarrassed to take the car into town – I couldn't stand all those people watching me.'
  Ridiculous? Try these:
  'Being able to sing is a gift of nature.'
  'I'll never be able to sing – it's just not in my genes!'
  'Sing? Either you can or you can't, and I can't!'
  'I love to sing in the shower, but I'd be too embarrassed to sing in public – I couldn't stand all those people hearing me.'
  What is the difference between the first and the second set of questions? Why do we assume that virtually everyone today is able to drive a car, but that singing is only for the chosen few? Why do we have expectations about the ability to sing that we do not have about driving? Why is singing a mysterious gift of nature while driving is merely something that most of us, at some stage, simply learn to do? We may choose not to learn to drive, but we seldom make the assumption that we lack the ability to do so.
  Yet singing used to be an ordinary pastime. Family and friends gathered around the piano in the evenings to sing. Musical evenings were a part of social life. Outdoor workers sang to the rhythm of their daily activities. Most communities had a local choir, and church choir stalls were filled with enthusiastic singers. Singing was part of daily life.

In the present day, singers are surrounded by an aura of mystery. Singers are idolised, often famous, often wealthy. They are not part of the familiar world of everyday. Have voices changed? Or is it merely that we have changed our assumptions about ourselves as singers?

Each of us probably has some ideal singer or ideal singing voice in our mind's ear when we sing. If the sound that comes out when we actually sing fails to approximate that ideal sound, we may feel that we ourselves have failed. But singing, like driving a car, or skiing, or playing chess, or managing a business, is a skill. To fulfil our potential, to reach the level of our ideal driver, skier, chess player, business manager or singer, we need knowledge, practice and experience. This book approaches singing from just that point of view. It provides factual knowledge about vocal technique and the musical skills required by the singer. It describes how to get the most out of singing practice sessions and gives information on further training.

How to use this book

Depending on what you are looking for, the book can be used in different ways. The second chapter shows the significance of mental attitude in learning how to sing. Drawing on ideas popularised by Neuro-Linguistic Programming, it introduces the idea that singers can use these skills to learn vocal technique and to prepare themselves for performances and other challenges. It explains the importance of mental conditioning in establishing muscle memory which creates the singing body.

The remaining chapters use these concepts as an approach to a comprehensive, precise and concrete guide to correct and healthy singing. Readers who want to know primarily about vocal technique – and this group may include parents and choral conductors as well as singers – can omit Chapter 2 and go straight to Chapters 3 and 4. Chapter 3 describes the mechanics of the singing voice from the physiological point of view and shows how the various parts of the vocal apparatus work, by themselves and in combination, to produce the singing voice. It also contains the basic vocabulary of singing terms. It discusses the role of the sound of the words – pronunciation – in the act of singing. Chapter 4, *Vocal Technique*, is the core of the book. Starting with the basics and going on to advanced techniques, it is a detailed, step by step programme of vocal instruction, complete with exercises, which discusses the aspects of breathing, resonance and interpretation, both individually and in relation to each other.

Chapters 5, 6 and 7 contain auxiliary information that will help the singing student get on in the world of music. Chapter 5, *Musical Skills*, gives advice on reading musical scores and how to learn a piece of music. Chapter 6, *Training the Voice*, will help those singers who are looking for a teacher. Chapter 7, *Singing Solo in Public*, gives the student a grasp of available opportunities, along with the tools needed to further goals in these areas. The final chapter, *Frequently Asked Questions*, answers questions that are asked time and time again by singers of all levels, school music teachers, choral conductors and parents of young singers.

I would like to say at this stage that for ease of reading on your part, I will not be tying myself in knots over politically correct inclusion of him/her in the text every time I mention students. Please assume that 'her' means equally 'him' and vice versa.

Chapter 2:

Thoughts about Singing

Athletes and others whose performance depends on peak physical and mental conditioning use various forms of mental preparation to enhance their competitive edge. Their practice sessions and their actual performances are likely to begin with a few quiet moments of visualisation during which they review their goals for that session and 'see' themselves successfully achieving those goals. They become adept at visualising perfect moves, slowing down their heart rate, blocking out distractions, calming nerves and even, to some extent, increasing their muscle tone without having to lift a finger! Learning physical and mental skills depends on establishing and consolidating pathways in the brain that will automatically and consistently make the connections that produce the result they want.

Like athletes, singers use the techniques of Neuro-Linguistic Programming (NLP) and coaching to help them improve their skills and reach their goals. A positive mental attitude, focus on technique and process rather than outcomes, and the silent practice of the music in real time, have been part of the singer's mindset for many years. Habitual use of these techniques eventually shifts the singer's 'knowledge' of her music from the conscious, thinking, mechanical, memorised stage to the subconscious state in which the musical expression has become spontaneous.

For example, a student expends thought and effort in learning the skill of making the leap from high A to the octave below on the two syllables, 'mu-sic'. This is a real challenge, since it involves singing a difficult consonant – the 'm' – on a high pitch and a difficult vowel sound – the 'u' – on a large leap through the *passaggio* between two registers (see Chapter 4). The singer perseveres with her thoughtful practice, and, over a period of time, the musical, mental and physiological path from the high to the lower octave, from the vowel 'u' to the 'i' via the 's', becomes established in her mind and body. Six months later, the singer encounters a similar octave leap, perhaps down from the upper A♭, on the word 'never'. Much of the work in learning how to sing the new bit of music has already been done. She does not have to go through a similar process, because the coordination of brain and muscle has evolved to the level of the subconscious, and the body – the voice – already knows how to sing it. The more connections the mind makes, the easier it becomes for the mind to make connections. This is the stage in which singing has finally become 'natural'. The mental, technical and physical aspects of the vocal process have become literally incorporated – this word means 'taken into the body'.

Singing, by its very nature, encourages concentration on goals. Singers strive to increase their range, sing longer phrases, sing more beautifully, win the competition, get great reviews, succeed at the audition. There are few professions as competitive as singing, and, even at the non-professional level, goal-setting, competitiveness and winning are 'part of the game'. Yet, so often, instead of providing themselves with the supportive, creative atmosphere that they need in order to learn and flourish, singers sometimes bombard themselves with negative thoughts that undermine their self-confidence.

The statements at the beginning of Chapter 1 are just such thoughts. Here are a few more:

'I'll never be as good a singer as she is.'

'I'm too old to learn.'

'I'll never be able to sing because I can't afford lessons.'

'I didn't have the right background, so I have all that against me.'

Constant repetitions of these assumptions lay down a foundation – a literal, neural network – of negative beliefs which entrap the singer and eventually keep her from moving ahead. If the singer who voiced these objections changed these assumptions (statements, beliefs) to those that follow, would her attitude, her commitment and the effort that she puts into her singing be different?

'I have unknown potential as a singer.'

'It's possible to learn to sing at any age.'

'I can learn a lot about singing from intelligent reading and listening.'

'My desire to learn how to use my voice is a measure of my ability to learn. It's a good thing that I have positive beliefs about myself and good learning habits.'

Studies have shown that 'high-achievers' have few negative presuppositions like the ones on the first list. Instead of allowing a negative thought to take hold and solidify into a belief, they replace it with a more open statement that embraces the possibility of a positive outcome. Then, by acting upon the positive belief, they increase their chances of fulfilling the outcome they desire.

How does this work in practice? Take this scenario as an example: a capable and diligent student came to her teacher in tears after an audition because, while she was singing, a group of singers (who should not have been present in any case) were rude about her performance. Naturally enough, the student was deeply hurt and resolved not to put herself in such a position again. The teacher made some enquiries and discovered that the other singers had mocked, not only this particular pupil, but all the entrants at the audition. When the teacher reported this to her student, the latter was able to replace her former assumption, 'I'm probably a poor singer because people laugh at me when I sing – I was stupid to try,' with the statement, 'Some people are just rude. I was happy with my performance and learnt a lot from the experience.' She shifted the focus of the problem away from herself onto the attitude of others while opening the incident to possibilities of growth. Now, each time this student sings in public, she builds upon a steadily growing base of self-knowledge and inner motivation, taking from the experience those aspects which will nurture her and her singing.

Many people tend to run scripts in their heads which are

based upon their memories and interpretations of past experiences. The student in this extreme example was setting herself up to run, over and over again, a script based on fears generated by an unpleasant experience. Instead, the student took action to interrupt the negative energy of the script – 'I'll never put myself in a position like that again' – which had locked her into her feelings of humiliation. She replaced it with a positive script that moved her forward – 'I thought I sang well, and I learnt something useful.'

Even singers who sing for pure enjoyment sometimes find themselves occasionally frustrated by stubborn technical challenges. For example, let's say that a soprano is working on a piece that contains a run from the G above middle C to the G one octave higher. She has managed to 'hit' the upper G during lessons with her teacher, but at home in the practice studio, as soon as she reaches the D, she feels her throat get tense and begin to close, even though she has warmed up. She finds herself lifting her shoulders and getting more and more tense as she sings higher and higher. By the time she gets to the F♯, she is very tense, she has run out of breath, her shoulders are up about her ears, she is pushing out sound, her throat is closing, and she is reaching, really reaching, for that top note. She is doing, in fact, all the things that her teacher has asked her not to do. The script that she is running in her head is the one that starts with the premise, 'This is difficult', 'It goes too high for me' or 'I can't sing that high.'

Yet the singer knows how to sing the phrase. She knows enough about singing technique, and about her own voice. She has, in fact, sung the phrase in her teacher's studio. Instead of thoughtlessly going over and over the phrase, she could take a few minutes to get herself into a frame of mind – quiet, receptive, curious – that would enable her to talk herself through this. She knows what to do. She knows how to take in the air, how to feel the expansion of the rib cage, to initiate the sound, to feel the throat opening as she continues the run though the passaggio, to feel the support working for her as she approaches the high note. In her imagination and in fact, she knows how to do everything she wants to do. She runs through this script a few more times in her head. She is replacing 'Oh, I can't do this' or 'Why bother anyway?' with the skill, knowledge and training that she already possesses. And in approaching the challenge in this way, she is creating and establishing the mental pathways and muscle responses that will consistently produce the outcome she desires.

In fact, singers learn partly by modelling the sounds they hear in their own minds. When someone is deeply absorbed in listening to a great tenor performing an aria (particularly one she already knows), she actually creates in her own body some of the same physiological and muscle effort that he is creating in his own. She is mimicking him. But the operative phrase here is 'deeply absorbed'. Playing an opera CD while she is making dinner may make her task more enjoyable, but will have little effect on her singing. Total absorption in the music, the feeling of 'being in the moment' while she is listening, will internalise some of the experience.

On a more precise and practical level, breaking down sounds into components is one way to model and instil specific sound-patterns. We can re-train ourselves to create the sensations that will consistently produce the sounds we wish to make. For example, many native English speakers have trouble pronouncing the German sound 'ü' (which is identical to the French 'u'). Yet if they are asked to say 'oo' and – without changing the position of their lips – say 'ee', they will produce the correct vowel sound. The singer has simply become aware of the steps involved in the making of the correct sound. By remembering the steps and repeating them, she will be able to produce the sound again. Eventually, she is able to make the sound without conscious thought. It has become unconscious because she has laid down the neural pathways and the muscle memory that enable her to reproduce the sound consistently.

When an individual learns a sport or any new skill that involves both mental and physical mastery and coordination, she trains mind and body equally. A singer learns her skill by becoming more aware of sensations which supply her with feedback about how she is singing. If she interrogates this feedback, she learns more quickly and more profoundly than she does if she merely continues to 'practise' unthinkingly.

Chapter 3:

Vocal Equipment

Vocal categories

Students often begin their training with misconceptions about the 'vocal category' to which they belong. 'I've always sung alto,' a choral singer will declare, 'because I can't hit anything higher than an E.' Another will claim to belong to no category, since he has been blessed with a huge range and he 'can sing anything'. Another young student feels more comfortable in the soprano register, but has been advised by the conductor of her choral group that she should 'go lower' since she is capable of singing the lower notes, and she'll get more solo work by doing so. The female singer of pop or rock music may not be aware that she possesses a head voice in addition to the chest voice she habitually uses.

The term 'vocal category' or 'vocal categorisation' is commonly used to describe types of voices. The four basic categories are the ones that are normally found in scores of choral music: soprano, alto, tenor and bass. These may be subdivided into soprano I and soprano II, alto I and alto II, and so on. These categories originally were used to differentiate each line of music in a vocal score from the others. Music that contains these vocal parts is scored, we say, for SATB, or SSATB, etc. Following this model, it has become common practice to ascribe the term 'vocal category' not merely to the vocal line, but to the singer who sings it. In other words, the singer's vocal type has become synonymous with the repertoire she most often sings. This may seem like an unimportant distinction. Unfortunately, it often misleads people into categorising their voices unnecessarily, prematurely or inaccurately.

Definitions of vocal categories

Soprano	Highest female voice.
	Also a young male treble voice (boy soprano).
Coloratura Soprano	Very high, flexible soprano voice, capable of great agility.
Dramatic coloratura	A voice that is equal to the coloratura in agility and the ability to sing high notes, but which has more dramatic weight and power, and is often darker in timbre, with a more substantial lower register.
	(For example, The Queen of the Night in Mozart's *The Magic Flute*.)
Soubrette	Light lyric soprano voice.
	(For example, Blonde and Despina in Mozart's *Così Fan Tutte*.)
Lyric Soprano	Soprano voice, bigger and usually somewhat darker than the above, suited to the lyric repertoire.
	(For example, Manon in Massenet's *Manon*.)
Lyric Coloratura Soprano	A voice that combines the warmth of the soprano voice with the height and flexibility of the coloratura soprano.
	(For example, Violetta in Verdi's *La Traviata*.)
Spinto Soprano	A darker, but still lyric, soprano, capable of greater power. The Italian term 'lirico spinto' means 'pushed lyric'.
Dramatic Soprano	Darkest of the soprano voices, one whose size or weight can be heard through the heavy orchestration of an opera by Wagner or Strauss.

Mezzo Soprano	A lower, darker and larger voice than the soprano.
Alto	The lowest of the female voices. Also used for lower boys' voices (boy alto). The terms 'alto' and 'contralto' are often used synonymously, for female voices only.
Countertenor	A male voice, sometimes called 'male alto', produced by the male falsetto.
Lyric Tenor	A lighter, high male voice with a characteristic 'ring' at the top of the range.
Dramatic Tenor (Wagnerian, heroic or Heldentenor)	Like the dramatic soprano, a weightier type of tenor voice with enough power to carry from the stage through a heavy orchestration.
High Baritone	An easy-to-listen-to voice characterised by its clarity and intelligibility in the middle register, with some of the baritone warmth and the tenor 'ring'. Many 'show voices' – voices which carry the narrative well in musical theatre – are high baritones.
Baritone	Between the tenor and the bass.
Bass-baritone	Between the baritone and the bass in terms of range and timbre.
Bass	A deep male voice, characterised by dark, rich and resonant sound with a slow vibrato.
Basso Profundo	The deepest male bass voice.

In operatic or classical music, the labels are even more numerous. The definitions on pages 16 and 17 are in general use, but they are both controversial and flexible. Ideally, they should be used only to describe a type of voice or a category of repertoire, rather than the singer herself. More often than not, it is counterproductive to try to fit a young singer into one of these particular categories at too early a stage.

Until their voices break, boys' voices are categorised as soprano or alto. The timbre and range of their voices before they break give no indication of the character of the voices after they break. For example, a boy alto may eventually become a tenor, a baritone or a bass.

When a student begins vocal study, she is often in a great hurry to 'find out' to which category she belongs. Even more so than in other skills, labelling oneself at an early stage of singing can be limiting. The character of each category depends upon a number of qualities – timbre, overtones and undertones, size and range. Since each voice is unique, placing the singer into a single category is often a difficult, and possibly unnecessary, task. Changes in these variables take place in the voice as the singer develops technical skill. They also depend on how much singing she does over a period of time, and on her age. For example, voices often become lower and darker with age; a 25-year-old lyric soprano may be singing as a mezzo when she reaches the age of 55.

Despite these reservations, however, it is usually necessary, at an advanced stage of study, to choose to move in the direction of a particular repertoire. This is not an easy task, and a singer who changes teachers or makes radical changes in her technique may encounter some resistance from her voice. It is not unusual for a novice student of 18 to be uncategorisable as a soprano or a mezzo. At 22, she may be considered a potential dramatic soprano. Two years later she may discover that the top register that she has never really used, along with a newly developed ability to sing florid coloratura music, opens a new repertoire to her – while closing another. The best advice is to remain flexible and constantly be aware of feedback from the voice. The question to ask is: how is the voice reacting to the choices that have been made for it?

Some young singers force the voice in a mistaken effort to make it bigger, louder or more powerful. Doing this will result, eventually and inevitably, in damage. A young voice should always be used lyrically; that is, lightly and with attention to the creation of a flowing melodic line. To use the voice dramatically means to add weight, power or darkening. Maturing voices can undertake this type of singing under the guidance of a knowledgeable teacher. A singer's continuous exploration and discovery of her unique voice and the repertoire associated with that voice is part of the process of learning to sing.

Singers at all levels and in all vocal categories do well to follow the principles of the 'Bel Canto' school, on which the technique in this book is based. Bel Canto simply means 'beautiful singing' in Italian. The old masters who developed and taught this technique in the eighteenth and early nineteenth centuries emphasised a flowing melodic line, beautiful sound and vocal agility, all of which depend upon the smooth and even production of an unforced but ringing tone.

Registration in the vocal categories

The concept of registration and its practical application to 'the blending of the registers' is dealt with in Chapter 4. It is introduced here because it is relevant to the thorough understanding of vocal categories.

The vocal categories are often used as a convenient way to classify a singer according to her vocal range. It would be more accurate to say that the vocal categories are terms for describing a type of voice based upon the character of its registration. 'Register' is a term used to describe the characteristic quality of a particular area of the voice. The usual terms are 'chest', 'head' and 'falsetto' for a man's voice, and 'chest', 'middle' and 'head' for a woman's voice.

The middle register is sometimes called the 'mixed' register. With study and practice, the head and the chest registers become blended so that the middle section of the voice demonstrates characteristics of both. At this stage, the voice, from the top to the bottom of the range, has a 'seamless' quality, and the changes from one register to another are almost, if not entirely, indiscernible.

Voice teachers and singers disagree on the number of registers in the human singing voice. A single register is considered to be the ideal; a fully trained voice possesses a unified quality throughout its range. Most teachers will base their technique on the concept of two registers – the head and the chest – and the need to blend them. This is the approach adopted by most professional singers, and by this book.

Whatever the approach of the teacher to registration, however, from the student's point of view the salient fact is this: many students at the beginning do not have any experience of singing in any register except the one in which they have always sung. Through experiment and practice the student may discover a part of her voice that she had been unaware of, or that she had discounted as 'weak' or 'unusable'. Through continuing exploration of the unfamiliar register and by learning to blend it with the one she is used to, she will discover that her vocal range has been considerably extended, and that the quality (character) of the voice may change. Only then will she able to place her voice, provisionally at least, into one of the above categories.

Vocal categories are characterised to some extent by vocal range. More important, however, is the balance of head and chest resonance that produces the characteristic sound quality of each category. The point is this: vocal training brings out the unique character of each voice by extending its range, flexibility and scope. Only when that character begins to develop in a recognisable direction should the singer attempt to place her voice into one of the vocal categories. Even then, she would be wise not to be overly rigid in her insistence on staying in that category.

Vocal range

If you have access to a piano at this point, it may make things easier to take a look at the keyboard, even if you do not play.

The octaves are numbered starting with C_1 being the lowest C on the keyboard, and going up to C_8. Generally speaking, the trained professional singer will have a usable range of two octaves or more. The range of the bass voice is from about E_2 below the bass staff to the E_4 above it. The range of the baritone voice will be about a third higher. The tenor will be able to sing from C_3 to the C_5 above middle C. For the female voices, the alto will be from the E_3 below middle C to the E_5. The compass of the mezzo voice will be from the G_3 below middle C to the G_5. That of the soprano voice will be from middle C (C_4) to high C (C_6). The coloratura soprano and basso profundo (deep bass) extend these ranges by as much a fifth in each direction.

These ranges are only general and, to some extent, arbitrary. Most professional singers extend these ranges in one direction by at least two or three tones beyond these limits. Voices which encompass three octaves are not rare. Some singers have three and one-half octaves in which they can make a proper 'singing' tone, although the usefulness of the extremes is variable.

Vocal categorisation depends as much upon timbre as upon range. Musical tones, including those produced by the singing voice, can be scientifically analysed in terms of the acoustical properties of their harmonic structure, including their overtones and undertones. The term 'timbre' is used to describe the effects of these properties in the voice (or other instrument). The word 'colour' is often used with the same meaning. Singers speak of, for example, warmth, purity, vibrancy or colourlessness in describing vocal timbre.

In addition, the *tessitura* of the music is a more significant feature than the actual range. The term 'tessitura', used in speaking of a particular voice or a specific piece of music, means the general range in which the voice usually sings. This means that the alto, with her low tessitura, sings mainly in chest or mixed tones, while the mezzo soprano, whose tessitura is a third higher, sings in mixed and head voice, and the soprano with the high tessitura sings almost exclusively in head voice. Corresponding registration is true for the tessiture of male voices.

Musical pieces are also said to have a high or low tessitura. For example, two pieces may have a range of a twelfth (say middle C to G_5). If most of the notes of the melody are in the lower part of this range, the song would be suitable for a mezzo; it is said to have a low tessitura. If most of the notes, however, are in the higher part of this range (that is, if its tessitura is high), it would normally be sung by a soprano.

This is the reason that transpositions of songs are not always successful. Transposing a piece of music from one key to another is one way of making a particular song, which may in its original be unsuitable for a particular singer's voice, accessible to her. For example, a song written for an alto may be transposed 'up a major second' to make it singable by a mezzo. Its low tessitura makes it suitable for either voice. If a soprano wished to sing it, however, merely transposing it up by a fourth, fifth or sixth will rarely make it singable for her, since the tessitura of the song will remain the same. Having said this, this example is an extreme case, and, with some manipulation, many songs can be transposed to suit individual voices.

This information may seem very confusing. In the early stages of singing, or if the singer is learning with the guidance of a knowledgeable teacher, it is perhaps more than the singer needs. Nonetheless, it is still important, for two reasons. First, once a singer begins to sing with a choir or light opera group or in a band, she should, for her own vocal health and safety, have some knowledge of her vocal strengths and limitations. This might mean, for example, being able to say 'no' if a conductor, desperate for altos, wants her to sing in the alto section just because she can manage to make a sound on the low notes. If the tessitura of the alto voice is too low to be comfortable for her, and she is comfortable and secure singing the high notes, she may reasonably expect that the soprano section is the place for her, at least at this stage of her singing progress. (Singers should not be frightened by this example! The purpose is not to demonise choral conductors, most of whom have the knowledge, experience and skill to help you make these choices.) As an example in a different type of music, it is easy to ruin a young, naturally powerful voice by asking the singer to push the chest notes higher and higher over a loud backup rock band. Being aware that each voice is different, and develops at its own pace, can help the singer make informed decisions about her musical environment.

The vocal apparatus

Like any other skill that places demands upon the body, singing uses a variety of anatomical systems. When these systems are working correctly and more or less automatically in coordination with each other, the singer has attained mental and physical control over her singing. In order to sing well, it is not necessary to understand all the precise and subtle movements of each set of muscles and each part of the body that is involved in the act of singing. It is, however, important to be able to use the correct terminology in order to talk about what is actually going on physically while we sing. Without this vocabulary, we have no framework on which to base our study and practice.

Two major aspects of singing technique are breathing and resonance. To create the sound you want, all the parts of the body that produce and control these two facets of sound production must work together in a coordinated fashion. For the purposes of discussion, the breathing apparatus will include explanations of the lungs, ribs and diaphragm. The concept of resonance will involve explanations of the areas of the face and throat which have an effect on the voice.

The underlying principle that informs the following discussion is that sound is actuated (or energised) by the breath, created in the vocal cords and given form in the resonating cavities. The unique character of each singer's voice is formed by the coordinated action of these three elements.

Breathing

The lungs are surrounded and protected by the rib cage. Between the ribs are two sets of intercostal muscles, the internal and the external. Expiration (exhalation, breathing out) is governed by the internal intercostals; they pull the ribs downward. Inspiration (inhalation, breathing in) is governed by the external intercostals; they pull the ribs upward. The two sets of muscles act together like a bellows to expand and contract the rib cage. In combination with other muscles in the thorax (the chest cavity), the intercostals allow the ribs to move up and down as well as out to the front, sides and back of the body.

The diaphragm is the main muscle of inspiration (breathing in). This large muscle separates the upper and lower parts of the human trunk. It is often thought of as the floor of the rib cage, to which it is attached. Above the diaphragm are the heart and lungs. In the relaxed position, it is high and dome-shaped. During inhalation, the diaphragm moves downward, as the capacity or volume of the lungs increases. With exhalation, the diaphragm moves upward and resumes its relaxed position.

The abdominal muscles (of the belly) tighten for exhalation. The action of these muscles is instinctive and we are generally not even aware of 'using' them, in the sense that we can easily become aware of 'using' the muscles of our fingers, for example, to type. Training them for singing requires, first of all, an awareness of these muscles and, secondly, a systematic approach to strengthening them and coordinating them with other processes. Chapter 4 looks at this in detail and includes exercises to improve awareness and use of muscles to support your singing.

The discussion on breathing has so far centred on the lungs, ribs and diaphragm. It is also possible to utilise the muscles of the shoulders in breathing. This is usually called clavicular breathing. If you have ever become 'out of breath' by running up a couple of flights of stairs, the chances are that you have found yourself resorting to the panting and the heaving chest that characterise clavicular breathing. A more subtle form of clavicular breathing is seen in nervous singers who take shallow, 'high', quick breaths in rapid succession. This has the effect of 'piling up' unusable, shallow breaths that prevent the singer's accessing the lower abdominal areas where she can support the breath. Clavicular breathing is to be avoided entirely.

The larynx is a muscular valve that closes off the top of the trachea, or windpipe, the air passage from the lungs to the mouth and nose. The lower folds of the larynx are called the vocal cords (not chords) and the space between them is the glottis. The epiglottis is a cartilage that drops down over the glottis during the act of swallowing to prevent food from entering the lungs. When it is not in use, the epiglottis is open to allow air to pass through. To create a speaking or singing sound (phonation), the vocal cords come together, causing resistance to the outflow of the breath. This produces the vibration that we call sound. When you sing (or speak aloud), what is travelling out of the mouth is not air, but sound energy.

The coordination of the muscles which control the breathing and those which control the larynx affects the quality of the singer's 'attack'. When the singer has taken a breath and begins the sound, the onset of the sound (attack) will be breathy if the opening and muscle tone of the cords are too loose. If the sound is initiated when the cords are already tightened, the attack will be harsh. Both extremes must be avoided. In the latter case, it is difficult, if not impossible, to relax the cords while phonation is still taking place. The effect on both listener and singer is uncomfortable, and prolonged or habitual singing with a tight larynx is both tiring and damaging.

Resonance

Resonance is the term given to the vibration produced by certain areas or cavities of the head and throat which add to the character and size of the sound that is produced in the larynx. To a large extent, the uniqueness of each human voice is due to the unique size, shape and surface texture of each individual's resonators. Part of the process – a largely unconscious part – of learning to speak, involves learning to coordinate the use of the dozens of muscles which control these areas in order to form consonants and vowels, and to provide tonal interest or expression to the words we speak. Just as each of us has learnt to control these muscles to modify, re-shape and change the size of the resonating cavities of the head and throat in order to speak, singers learn to use the resonators to form words as well as to control the amount and kind of resonance in their singing voices. Some of this muscular control is amenable to conscious manipulation, in much the same way that a riding instructor can tell a rider how to hold her reins correctly. Soon the rider picks up the reins correctly without having to think about it. However, because the muscles that control the voice are both numerous and invisible, often it is more useful to speak about them using imagery. Nonetheless, it is important to define terms at this stage so that the discussion on resonance in Chapter 4 will be intelligible.

The resonators that concern singers are the throat, the mouth, the sinus cavities and the nose. The bones of the head are also often thought to add resonance.

The throat, or pharynx, is the space above the larynx (voice-box) and behind the mouth cavity. Of all the resonating cavities, it is the one most amenable to conscious control, and a large part of the singer's effort goes into learning, first of all, what the throat should be doing during the act of singing, and secondly, into habituating the throat to performing these actions automatically. Singing with an open throat produces the rich, mellow undertones that we think of as 'resonance'.

The use of the term 'mouth' can lead to some confusion, since the word refers both to the oral cavity and to the orifice formed by the lips. This discussion uses the term to refer to the resonating oral cavity. When the throat is open, it automatically seems to form a single resonating chamber with the mouth, and like the throat, the mouth can be altered in size and shape. These alterations, caused by changes in the tongue, teeth, lips, soft palate and jaw position, form vowels and consonants. The singer's task is to articulate words without disturbing the quality and the flow of sound which has been formed in the larynx and whose resonance is taking place in the open throat. Singers often find it frustrating when they 'add the words' to a song which they had previously been vocalising on 'ah', and find that the quality of the sound has been affected by the action of the mouth in forming words. Again, the singer needs to acquire the skill of making the words intelligible while maintaining a resonant sound.

Vowels and consonants are formed in the mouth by changes in its boundaries – the teeth, tongue, lips, cheeks, hard palate and soft palate. The hard palate forms the roof of the mouth. The soft palate forms the extension of the hard palate at the back of the mouth. The soft palate is also known as the velum, although this term may also refer to only the extreme lower edge of the soft palate. The uvula is the small bit of muscle tissue that hangs down in the centre of the soft palate.

The sinus cavities lie behind the cheekbones on either side of the nose. There is controversy over whether or not these cavities are actually responsible for any part of the resonance in the human voice, and certainly any resonance that takes place in this area is not controlled by voluntary muscle action. Nonetheless, the imagery that singers use to 'place the sound in the facial mask' is unquestionably effective, and it is equally true that singers 'feel resonance' or 'buzzing' or 'tickling' in this area when they have achieved the desired resonant qualities in their voices.

The same is true of the nose. The notion of nasal resonance is used as a means of gaining control over placement. As an experiment, try making a forward, open, singing sound and, without changing the sound at all, pinch your nostrils together. The sound probably does not (it should not) change at all. Again, the sensation of tickling or buzzing in the nose while singing may indicate that sympathetic vibrations are being set up in the area, and thinking of the nose as part of the facial mask to which the singer directs her sound can be a useful image.

Singing in the nose (that is, singing nasally) should always be avoided. The French nasal vowels do not need to be sung in an exaggeratedly nasal way if the tone is already correctly placed in the mask. The nasal sounds in English, 'm', 'n' and 'ng', are often used in vocalising to help place the sound forward. Again, the nasality of these tones should be de-emphasised and the concept of 'forward placement' used instead. Finally, using the French 'on' in the passaggio is an effective way of bringing the sound forward while simultaneously opening the throat. This may help to bring a 'ring' into this part of the voice.

A singer will probably feel the tone in the nose, but there should never be an overtly nasal sound in that tone. If the sound has a nasal quality to it, the singer is actually cutting off mouth resonance. To experiment with this, sing a nasal 'ee'. While singing, drop the jaw, opening the mouth wide.

It is arguable whether the bones of the head participate in the resonance produced by the singing voice. Singers often feel sympathetic vibration in the forehead. The jaw may occasionally be felt to vibrate also, although this may be an effect of singing certain vowels at a medium pitch ('e' for example). The jaw, if it is tight or rigid, can interfere with resonance.

The vocal mechanism and the singing voice

Just as the knowledge and practice of balanced posture is essential to the singer's breathing and support, an understanding of how the resonating chambers and the bones of the head produce the sound will help to rid these areas of tension and constriction so that the voice can be produced freely. Much of the actual technique of singing is based upon the need to keep the pronunciation of the words from interfering with the production of the tone. Paradoxically, the pronunciation can be used to free the tone and enhance the sound.

Vowels

All singing takes place on the vowels. If you prolong the voicing of any vowel, you will be singing that vowel. Try saying the word 'no' and continue the 'o' sound, and you will see this for yourself. For the singer's purposes, words consist of vowels, which 'carry' the sound (a, e, i, o, u, in English), plus consonants, which are used for articulation. If I say the word 'cake', you know what I mean, but if I simply say 'ay' (the sound of the vowel in 'cake') you can't tell whether I wish to say 'cake', 'made', 'tale' or another single syllable word containing that sound.

The theory of the formation of sounds in speech is the province of the science of linguistics. A basic *practical* knowledge of their formation will help the singer free her sound from the tyranny of having to pronounce words as if she were speaking them. To create various vowel sounds, the mouth changes shape and the larynx changes position. Try this exercise. Start by saying 'ah' and note the position of the tongue. It is probably lying on the floor of the mouth. Say 'oh'. The tongue remains flat, but the lips become slightly pursed. Now say 'oo'. The jaw probably rises slightly, the lips are pursed and the larynx drops. Say 'ah' once more, and note the position of the tongue. Now say 'ay'. The front of the tongue rises and moves slightly forward. Now say 'ee'. The larynx rises. Say 'ee' and 'eh' several times, to feel the places where the vowels are created and the changes that they make within the internal spaces of the mouth and pharynx.

In addition to these five vowels, of course there are many other vowel sounds in English (both British and American English) and in other languages. Singing in French requires careful placement of the nasal vowels. Singing in German offers the challenge of the umlaut, as well as, ideally, the ability to differentiate between the tense and the lax forms of certain vowel sounds. This distinction exists also in English, where long (tense) and short (lax) vowels ('feat' and 'fit', for example) form part of the range of sounds. In Italian, care must be taken to produce the pure Italian vowels and vowel groups, not merely their English approximations or sloppy misrepresentations. To sing in any language, including her native English, the singer must have her mind and her ears open. She cannot afford to carry, unthinkingly, all her notions and habits of pronunciation of speech over into her singing. Nor can she be insensitive to the different repertoire of sounds that she will need to produce in order to sing in other languages.

The singer who wishes to sing the classical repertoire,

whose native language is English, whether she is British, North American, Australian or from any other part of the English-speaking world, will find it necessary at some stage to come to grips with both the meaning and the pronunciation of foreign languages. As far as pronunciation goes, she can get away, at least in the initial stages, with listening to native singers and with working with a language coach or knowledgeable singing teacher. Many English-speaking singers despair over this fact. However, her innate ability to mimic sounds will prove useful in this regard; one of the best ways to learn how to pronounce a foreign language is to listen to native singers. Another thing to remember is that all people, no matter what their native language, have basically the same vocal equipment and, therefore, the same ability to create the sounds of any language. We are limited by our habit of speaking one language, which leads us to believe that we are capable of forming only the set of sounds associated with that language. Finally, the rules of pronunciation of French, German, Italian and Spanish, as well as most other languages, have few exceptions and can be easily learnt, while for non-native speakers, English is notoriously the most difficult foreign language to pronounce, since there are as many exceptions to the rules of English pronunciation as there are rules themselves – and you have already mastered all of these.

The dipthongs in English are double vowel sounds that occur on a single (written) vowel. For example, the word 'I' is a dipthong, consisting of the two sounds 'ah' and 'ee'. (As a contrasting example, the word 'beat' contains two vowels, but no recognisable dipthong – only the single 'ee' sound.) French and Italian use dipthongs very little, if at all. In general, when singing in English, all the vowel sounds should approximate the Italian. Dipthongs present a special case in which convention, taste and style all play a part. These considerations make generalisation difficult, as the following examples will illustrate.

In general, when singing in a 'classical' style, the tonal and temporal emphasis will be on the initial component of the dipthong. The English letter 'i' is pronounced with a dipthong by native speakers of English: 'ah-ee'. While this is perfectly correct, it should be minimised when sung. When singing the word 'idle', for example, the first sound should be 'ah', and the 'ee' should be merely touched immediately before the voice moves to the following syllable. The two elements of the dipthong should be sung deliberately; that is, the 'ah' must not anticipate the 'ee' but, when the change is made, it must be made precisely, quickly and subtly. The audience must never be aware of what is happening.

Take the word 'music', however. This word contains a special kind of dipthong called 'the glide' or 'ee-oo'. The word will sound very strange if the singer elongates the initial 'ee' of the first syllable and touches the 'oo'. To sing this dipthong, she should sing 'mee-oo', getting rid of the initial 'ee' as quickly as possible and singing on the 'oo'.

Style is, however, another consideration. Musical examples of songs in which pop singers or crooners elongate the 'ee' in 'I' are numerous. And 'you', which would be sung as the un-dipthongised Italian 'oo' in an English classical song, is sometimes produced as 'you-ah' in Big Band music. Musical examples abound, and the singing student would do well to listen to a variety of styles of music to familiarise herself with the different conventions and stylistic nuances of each, paying close attention to the treatment of the vowel sounds. To substitute one usage for another is to betray a lack of awareness or care, and the audience, adjudicator or agent will not tolerate it.

In Italian, the purity of the vowels is one of the factors responsible for its 'singability'. One of its difficulties for the native English speaker is, however, the sheer number of words and phrases in which pure vowels follow one another thick and fast, all of which must be given their due, even when sung rapidly. For example, the Italian possessive adjective 'miei' contains three separate and distinct pure vowel sounds, none of which may be glossed over or emphasised. Frequent mistakes are made in the actual pronunciation of 'io', 'tuo' and particularly 'lui'. In each case, the first and second vowels are pronounced separately and distinctly from each other. 'Io' must be 'ee-oh', not 'yo'. 'Tuo' is 'too-oh', not 'twoh'. And 'lui' is almost invariably pronounced by English singers who have studied a bit of French as 'lwee'; its correct Italian pronunciation is 'loo-ee'. Again, the singer who takes the trouble to consult an Italian language text which contains the rules of pronunciation, and to learn and practise those rules will not go wrong when she encounters the words 'gli occhi', or anything else.

Articulation (consonants)

Singing, then, takes place on the vowels and vowel sounds. When singers 'vocalise' a song – when they sing only on vowels – there is nothing to interrupt the flow of beautiful sound. Some composers have even written songs without words, called 'vocalises', so that the sound of the human voice can be appreciated as an instrument like any other. The purely instrumental aspect of the voice is largely responsible for its expressive quality, which must be preserved when the singer has words to sing!

The sound of the human voice in singing is, of course, beautiful and, more importantly, it is expressive. The voices of singers from Pavarotti to Elvis Presley, from Cecilia Bartoli to Shirley Bassey, have in common the ability to convey human emotion directly through their expressive quality. Like great actors, these singers are capable of acting 'with their voices'; that is, of creating mood, emotion and empathy, of setting up human resonances that we all respond to. There is another dimension to the sound of the singing, or speaking, voice, and that is, of course, the fact that vowels form only a part of words. Words are expressive in two ways. We respond to the sound of the word, just as we respond to the sound of the human voice singing it. We also respond to the meaning of the word. The singer sometimes looks upon the consonants (that, with the vowels, constitute words) as nuisances, since they interfere with the production of the singing sound – they interrupt the flow of the vowel sound. Nevertheless, the consonants, when they are properly understood by the singer and incorporated into her vocal technique, are an important tool to convey meaning. Chapter 4 contains a discussion of the technical aspects of dealing with consonants. Here the formation of some different types of consonants is related to their role in singing.

1.   SEMI-VOWELS

Some consonants are semi-vowels. These are 'l', 'm', 'n' and 'r'. Like vowels, they make a continuous sound – you can sing on them. But unlike vowels, they are produced with the mouth partly or completely closed. Try singing any of these semi-vowels; then, without stopping the sound, open your mouth, and you will see that they change to some real vowel, usually 'ah'.

(a)   'l' and 'r'

When sung, the 'l' and the 'r' can cause particular difficulties to the native English speaker if they are pronounced gutturally (that is, in the back of the throat). There are many different ways of pronouncing these particular consonants in standard English, and American English gives additional scope for back pronunciation.

Forming these consonants in the back of the throat not only strangles the phonated, energised flow of air (on the vowel), it also distorts the vowels that precede and follow it. Finally, the 'l' and the 'r' which are formed in the back of the throat require a massive re-configuration of the tongue and throat, and take, in terms of simply getting the words out, rather a long time.

The general rule must be to allow the 'l', when sung in any language, including English, to approximate closely the corresponding Italian consonant, since the latter is pronounced at the teeth, rather than in the back of the throat. This means that the 'l' should be pronounced by flipping the tip of the tongue against the back of the top teeth. To experience this feeling, and to practise it, sing 'la, la, la', etc., with the jaw dropped (the mouth open). This exercise exaggerates the necessary movement by causing the tongue almost to flip out of the mouth, but it will give you the sensation of forming the 'l' behind the teeth rather than in the back of the throat.

The 'r' is rather more complicated. The spoken 'r' in French, German, Italian, English, Scottish and American is pronounced uniquely in each language. A mispronounced 'r', sung in any of these languages, is a 'dead giveaway' of the foreign singer. When singing in the English, the English 'dropped r' should be used when it is followed by other consonants or consonant sounds ('earth', 'form', 'forth', 'foretell'). When the 'r' is followed by a vowel sound or stands alone (as at the end of a word), English should approximate the Italian 'r' with a single 'flip' of the tongue at the alveolar ridge. To try this, say the sound 'd'. Now say the sound 'r' in exactly the same place. When used in English, this roll must never become excessive, although you may hear a rolled 'r' on some pre-1950 recordings. It should be noted that, in Italian, the 'r' is actually rolled (that is, the tongue flutters against the alveolar ridge), whereas when it is used in English, the tongue merely touches it in a single flutter.

The 'r' in spoken French and German is produced at the back of the mouth by the fluttering of the uvula against the back of the tongue. In French art song and opera, the rolled 'r' is always used as a substitute (by native French speakers themselves), although the velar or uvular 'r' is usually used in popular songs. In sung German, the rolled 'r' is used by German singers as an acceptable substitute for the guttural 'r', although the latter is perfectly correct, as long as it does not interrupt or distort the production of the accompanying vowels.

The American retroflex 'r', which is produced by curling the tip of the tongue backwards, produces a corresponding backward slide of the entire tongue into the throat. It has no place in classical vocal technique, and is usually avoided in favour of either the English 'dropped r' or the Italian rolled or flipped 'r', as appropriate. It can be used for particular effects, but, in general, it is best avoided.

(b)   The nasals – 'm', 'n', and 'ng'

Like the 'l' and the 'r', the nasals are semi-vowels. Like vowels, the characteristic of their production is glottal vibration, sustained for the period of their voicing. The nasals are 'm', 'n' and the sound 'ng', as in 'singing'. To produce a true vowel, however, the mouth must be open, and to produce the nasals, the mouth is closed. The resonance that is produced takes place in both the mouth and the nose.

Although humming on the 'm' and the 'n' is often used as an exercise by the singer to 'place the sound forward', the nasality of these consonants should never be carried over into singing words. The phrases 'feeling the buzz', 'feeling the vibration', or 'feeling the tickle' in the nose and the areas to either side describe the sensation of 'putting the sound in the facial mask'. Singing in any language should not sound nasal. If it does, you are cutting off mouth resonance.

In French, a vowel followed by 'n' or 'm' causes that vowel to become nasalised; under these circumstances, having fulfilled its unique function as the cause of the nasalised vowel, it is not itself pronounced. Some singers mistakenly nasalise the vowel and then pronounce the following nasal consonant as well. For example, singers should pronounce the nasal 'o' in 'le monde' but not the 'n'. With the exception of the usage of these consonants to nasalise vowels, French is no more nasal than any other language, and the singer who adds a nasal quality in circumstances other than these is mistaken.

The nasals in Italian, English and German should not be emphasised. Singers should note that the English 'ng' sound does not exist in Italian. The 'ng' in 'languisce' must not be pronounced like the 'ng' in English 'languish'. Rather, the 'n' and the hard 'g' must be pronounced separately, 'lan-guisce'.

2.   THE GLOTTAL STOP

Remember that the glottis is the space between the vocal cords. If a vowel sound is initiated while the glottis is still closed, a glottal plosive – also called a hard attack – is the result. In fact, the attack is similar to the beginning of a cough or a laugh. Although it is generally considered to be correct in spoken French or German, it is usually avoided by native singers of those languages. The sound is harsh, and the effect on the vocal cords more so. In English, it should be avoided altogether.

Most singers seem to be aware of this to some degree when the question is one of initial vowels, but are unaware of the 'glottal stop' that replaces the 't' in much British and American speech. The tendency of almost all speakers is to substitute the 't' with a glottal stop. For example, in the phrases 'that boy', 'Great Britain', 'sat down', each 't' sound at the end of the first syllable will almost invariably be lost as a glottal stop, and many inexperienced singers would automatically sing the phrases in the same way. In each case, however, the 't' should be pronounced perfectly distinctly, while simultaneously linking it with legato to the following word. This may produce the illusion of an added syllable, where 'sat down', for example, becomes 'satuhdown'. This is preferable to the use of the glottal stop, but must itself be minimised.

Conclusion

The preceding paragraphs have provided only a few examples of common pitfalls in pronunciation and some pointers or suggestions in how to avoid them. As a musician, the singer is in the unique position of having an instrument that is capable of producing a legato (connected, seamless, smooth sound) that is virtually perfect, while the fact that she needs to sing words effectively prevents her from doing so. Nevertheless, she must remember that the ideal is 'to keep the sound going'; that is, to create the illusion of continuous resonance despite the repeated interference of consonants. It is the words, after all, that carry the meaning as well as the expression of the emotion.

Chapter 4:

Vocal Technique

Singing and athleticism

If you think back to a time when you first took up a sport, or when you had your first driving lesson, perhaps you remember having felt uncoordinated and awkward. You understood the instructor's directions, but as soon as you tried to put them into practice, 'the whole thing fell apart'. You grasped the mental processes of performing the necessary physical actions, but, until the smooth, coordinated movements had worked themselves into your muscle memory, there seemed to be a huge gap between the concept and the performance. With practice and experience, however, it all seemed easy.

Singing is exactly the same. We think of singing as an art and as a gift. This is true, but singing is also a highly athletic use of the body which demands instantaneous physiological responses to conscious and unconscious mental processes. The singer has gained some skill when these activities have become coordinated through training and experience. Like the advanced skier, the advanced singer is always thinking ahead, reading the terrain and staying in touch with her body. Her mind and her body make coordinated use of the technique that has become second nature to her.

Although many people think that singing is purely aural, analysis proves this notion misleading. Of course the singer and her audience both hear the sounds that she is singing. But let's work back from this. Before she produces the sound, she has to know how to produce it. And in order to know what kind of sound she wants to produce, she has to have an image (idea, mental picture) of that sound.

To understand what this means, sing any note and actively listen to it. Is there anything you can do to the sound once it has been sung? No, it's too late. The only way to exercise control over the sound is to train your body to perform the appropriate actions, which will in turn produce the sound you want. Hearing music is an aural activity; singing music is an imaginative and a kinaesthetic (physical) activity.

In order to sing, the singer must train, or condition, her body to produce a consistent set of responses to her mental instructions. It is possible to control many of the muscles that work together to produce singing. The diaphragm and the other muscles that we use for support can be controlled in such a way. Others, like the muscles that are used to form the various vowel sounds, are not usually controlled directly. Singers approach the use of these muscles through the use of imagery.

How to use this chapter

This chapter is designed to be used by singers at any stage of their vocal development. The elements of singing technique are explained step by step, each stage building upon familiarity with the preceding ones. If you have taken singing lessons in the past, or if you are working now with a singing teacher, you can easily use the sectional headings to help you find information on specific topics, or you may prefer to approach the chapter according to the following recommendations. If you have not taken singing lessons before, this is the recommended way to read this chapter:

(i) Read the whole chapter through without stopping to do the exercises. Then, to use this chapter as the basis for learning how to use correct technique in singing, proceed as in steps (ii) to (vi) below. Keep in mind section 8 (The practice session) and section 9 (Vocal strain) while you are working. Section 8 contains a model practice session. Section 10 (Style) may answer some questions about the compatibility of vocal technique with various styles of singing.

(ii) Read sections 1 (Balance and posture) and 2 (Breathing) together and practise the exercises for a couple of days until you feel that you have gained some control over the muscular responses required by these activities.

(iii) Building on what you have learnt in sections 1 and 2, read section 3 (Support) and practise the exercises for a few days.

(iv) Read section 4 (Placement and resonance) and section 5 (The vocal registers) together. Again, practise these exercises for a few days.

(v) Add section 6 (Colour). Again, practise these exercises for a few days.

(vi) Add section 7 (Phrasing). Some of the flexibility exercises are quite demanding. Less advanced students should omit these.

1.   Balance and posture

Good posture produces several conditions necessary to the act of singing. First of all, the singer will be dynamically balanced. Secondly, the muscles which support the sound will be free of unproductive tension. Thirdly, the organs and other apparatus which produce the sound will be free of constriction.

It is important to note that good posture does not mean stasis or rigidity. While concert singers usually stand facing the audience throughout a performance, singers of opera, musical theatre or pop and rock music often move about, sometimes very energetically. The principles and physical aspects of good posture are the same whether the singer is standing still or moving about.

For the novice singer, however, and during the practice session at any level, it is recommended that a quiet, balanced and poised stance be adopted and maintained. Movement of the arms and hands, or shifting the weight from foot to foot, or walking about, must be avoided. These actions sometimes originate as nervous habits or a wish to 'express the music'.

They have no place in practice, and merely use up physical and mental energy. Above all, do stand up! Sitting down during any stage of practice may inhibit your understanding and learning of these techniques. If you refer to this book frequently while you are working through the instructions or the exercises, place it at head level on a music stand. Focus your eyes at a place on the wall or look straight out the window while practising these or any other exercises. The distortion of sensation (and sound) that you cause by looking down – if the book is lying open on a table, for example – will render the exercises useless. By the same token, looking up or twisting the head to one side will also distort the sound. The gaze should be parallel to the floor.

Remain aware of the body during practice: it is the instrument you are playing. Using a mirror as you work through the following instructions will help with this. Done properly, the singing posture looks and feels both natural and relaxed. Keep adjusting the body and refining the posture until this has been achieved.

Stand with feet a little less than hip distance apart, toes facing forward. The weight is equally distributed between the two feet. The weight is also equally distributed between the heel and the ball of each foot. Maintenance of this posture will preclude rocking from side to side and from front to back. Singers sometimes try to 'reach' for high notes by raising themselves on their toes. It won't work!

The hips are slightly 'open', but not rigidly so. This will engage the muscles of the legs to the correct degree. Be careful, however, not to arch the back. The pelvis remains in line with the legs, neither tipped forward excessively nor thrust towards the back. Take a look at yourself in the mirror from the side to check this aspect of your posture.

The upper part of the body is upright. Have the feeling that there is an invisible string attached to the top of the head, lifting the body gently upwards.

The shoulders are down and slightly back. This has the effect of 'opening' the chest, but, again, be careful not to arch the back or to thrust the chest forward. The arms and hands are relaxed and hanging quietly at the sides of the body. One of the most common errors of posture, even among experienced singers, is tension in the shoulders and upper arms. The shoulders of many singers tend to creep up towards the ears. Practising in front of a mirror will help to avoid this problem.

The head is balanced at the centre of the body between the shoulders. The gaze is directed straight ahead, parallel to the floor. In effect, this means that the head is not tilted up or down or to one side.

2.   Breathing

A great deal is known about the physiology of the breathing apparatus. Singing students who are interested in detailed anatomical aspects of voice production can find plentiful information in books or on the Internet. In the early stages, and, indeed, for all practical purposes, knowing how all the muscles and organs work is largely irrelevant. We all 'know how' to breathe, and learning how to breathe for singing involves nothing more than making slight changes to a perfectly natural activity that all of us perform.

When we inhale, the lungs fill with air. This causes the rib cage to expand. Most of the action is not visible, but you can feel what is happening to a certain extent. Stand in front of a mirror, preferably with this book propped on a music stand that is raised to head level. Look in the mirror and take a slow, deep breath. You will see the rib cage expanding. It expands to the front and the sides, and may also expand to the back. While this is happening, the diaphragm, a powerful muscle which separates the chest cavity from the abdomen, flattens. It is possible to feel the action of the ribs, and, to a limited extent, the result of the movement of the diaphragm. Place the tips of the fingers of one hand on your chest just below the breast-bone. Place the other hand flat against your side. Breathe deeply and slowly, without exaggeration, and you will feel the expansion of the ribcage.

The inhalation must be deep, even and slow, giving the illusion of 'breathing into the belly'. Taking a quick, shallow breath will only result in 'chest breathing'. In this case, the singer's upper chest and shoulders rise up. This type of breathing cannot produce a good tone or a long phrase.

The chest remains open during exhalation. Neither the chest nor the shoulders should be allowed to collapse forward. If your chest and shoulders tend to collapse, try standing against a wall and practise breathing into the belly. When you are singing, maintaining good posture throughout the practice will reinforce this important habit.

The following exercises will help you to increase awareness and control of the muscles. The first demonstration shows you how to feel the coordinated action of the diaphragm and the lower abdominal muscles (which lie below the waist, between the pelvic bones). Lie flat on the floor with your legs stretched out in front of you and your arms lying at your sides. Place two or three books on the abdomen over the waist area (between the pelvic bones and the rib cage). When you inhale properly, you'll feel the books lift. When you exhale, you'll feel the books dropping down again.

A second breathing exercise will strengthen the muscles. Stand up for this one, and check that your posture is correct. Open the mouth and let the lips and tongue remain relaxed. Inhale deeply but quickly and then pant like a dog, using the lower abdominal muscles. Be careful to inhale and exhale each time. (If you inhale just once and then just expel the air in short puffs, you are not exercising the full set of muscles.) It is not necessary to exaggerate this movement. Simply allow the natural action of the diaphragm to do its work. Keep the panting rhythmical. You may change the tempo, making it faster or slower, but don't let the exercise get out of control. While you are panting, focus your attention on the abdominal muscles.

Breath control

Breath control is normally thought of as the ability to sing longer and longer phrases without 'running out of air'. For the novice student it often seems like the most important aspect of singing, although 'having more power' comes a close second.

Ultimately, true control of the breath depends on the coordination of the breathing with the specific phrase that is being sung. That is, breath control in singing, as in speaking, is contextual. Each phrase of vocal music is unique, and an experienced singer will use the breath to express the meaning of the phrase she is singing. The control of the breath for singing eventually becomes automatic, spontaneous and natural. At that point, all concerns about 'control' disappear.

In the beginning, it is far more important to use the breath wisely than to worry about sustaining long phrases. Having said that, correct use of the muscles from the early stages of singing study is essential to the mental coordination of breath control with breath support, and continued thoughtful practice will inevitably increase the strength, flexibility and precision of the muscles that are involved in breathing.

The most important consideration is dynamic posture. Inexperienced or untrained singers often allow the chest to collapse or sink inward during exhalation. If you try this in front of a mirror, exhaling by deliberately allowing the chest to collapse and the shoulders to come forward while vocalising on 'ah', you will see and hear the result: a sound that is pushed or breathy, or both. By contrast, stand in front of the mirror, take a good breath and sing 'ah' while keeping the chest open as if you were not expelling any air at all. As you expel the air, you should feel (a) a natural contraction of the muscles of the lower abdomen. You may also feel (b) the pelvis 'tucking in' slightly. (Be careful, however, not to allow the back to become arched.) Both actions are entirely correct and do not need to be exaggerated or done deliberately. The sound that is produced is both controlled and supported; this sound forms the basis of correct and healthy singing.

Remember: for singing, the chest must be open during both inhalation and exhalation.

Because singing is a physical activity that requires high levels of energy and cardiovascular fitness, singing students will benefit from regular training in sports or other physical activities. Pilates and power (Astanga) yoga are particularly recommended for their positive effects on posture and musculature through emphasis on breath management, concentration and body awareness. Running, cycling, rowing, step, circuits or any other sport which challenges and increases cardiovascular fitness is fine as long as the activity does not produce a superabundance of phlegm and persistent sore throat, coughs or colds, an occasional side-effect of such sports.

Exercises to increase awareness and control of the breath

(a) Inhale slowly through the nose while counting to five; exhale through the nose while counting to eight or ten. This can be practised anywhere for any length of time. Gradually increase the count. Keep the chest open the whole time.

(b) Inhale quickly but deeply through the nose; exhale slowly through pursed lips, 'spinning out' the breath for as long as possible. Again, keep the chest open and maintain good posture throughout the exercise.

This quick intake of breath is sometimes called a 'surprise breath'. If done correctly, it has the effect of producing the ideal adjustment of both throat and lower abdominal muscles. To experiment with this, take the 'surprise breath' and hold it for a moment, noticing the slight 'set' of the lower abdominals and the relaxed openness of the throat. This gives you some idea of the 'inner posture' that allows the singer to support the breath. (Note: under normal circumstances you will never hold your breath during singing practice.)

A word of caution: singing soon after eating a full meal may feel very uncomfortable and will almost certainly inhibit your breathing and support.

3. Support

The term 'support' is used by singers to describe the conscious control of the air pressure within the thoracic cavity (the chest). Its purpose is to produce 'a singing tone', rather than one which is breathy or weak. By engaging certain muscles that modify the air pressure, the singer consciously slows down and controls the outflow of the air during the act of singing. Every individual sound and every phrase must be 'supported by the breath'.

If you have done the exercises in the last section on breath control, you will have already become aware of the activity of the muscles of the lower abdomen. Support builds on the awareness and control of these muscles.

The following experiment will help you to feel the sensation that is meant by the term 'support'. Read through this paragraph and get the steps into your mind before you try it; the actions of imagining, inhalation, supporting and phonation (the making of the sound) have to flow into one another. Unless you are specifically asked to do so, at no point in any of these exercises should you hold your breath!

The thoracic cavity is the area within the rib cage, where the lungs do their work. As you slowly inhale, think of having a balloon inside the body which extends from the thoracic cavity all the way down into the lower part of the abdominal cavity. The rib cage will expand *outwards* as you inhale. (As always, it is very important not to let the chest or shoulders rise.) The lower abdomen will expand *outwards* also. Now imagine that you are not going to allow the balloon within your body to release any of the air which it contains. In practice, this means that the chest will remain expanded as if filled with air (not collapsing) and that the lower abdomen will remain pushed out (not relaxing). Although you are about to exhale, you will continue to hold your body, internally and externally, in the position of maximum inhalation. Keeping this in mind, sing (on any comfortable pitch), the vowel 'ah' for a few seconds, concentrating your awareness of the sensations in the chest and down into the lower abdomen. Notice the sound that you are making, but do not concentrate your attention on it.

If you have done the experiment successfully, you will have noticed that the muscles of the lower abdomen remain engaged throughout the whole process of expiration. This feeling is, essentially, the sensation of 'supporting the breath'.

If you have never experienced the sensation of breath support, it can seem like a lot of work. With practice, however, the muscular and mental coordination of the process becomes habitual and the process itself will seem natural and automatic. In Italian, the sensation is called 'appoggio', which means 'leaning into'. You may have the feeling of 'leaning into' the muscles of the lower abdomen as you vocalise on the vowel. Be careful, however, not to sing too loudly; this is counter-productive and can be injurious, especially to young singers.

To establish a continuous feeling of support while you are doing your singing practice, or to check that you are actually supporting properly while you sing, try this. Stand facing an immovable object, with your abdomen firmly touching it. A grand piano is ideal, since your feet go under the cabinet and your upper body (and your voice) are not obstructed, but a filing cabinet or even the wall will do. When you take the breath (as above) push gently into the piano with the abdomen. You should find that the body is being pushed away from the piano by the gentle action of the inhalation.

A word of caution: have the feeling that the *abdomen* is pressing against the object as you sing, but be very careful not to have the feeling that you are pushing out air by applying pressure directly to the *larynx* (the voice-box)! This sensation must be avoided at all times.

To gain awareness of the sensation of support, practise these visualisation techniques. They are used by singers at every stage of their development to re-establish the feeling of support or to check that they are supporting properly. Correct support feels like this:

(a) Have the feeling that the air you have taken in is enclosed in a big rubber beach ball. When you exhale or sing, your task is to keep the beach ball underwater.

(b) Have the feeling of gently bearing down.

(c) Until recently, some singers actually wore tight corsets or belts to assist this sensation of support or 'appoggio'.

Wearing such garments is not recommended, as they will only constrict the organs. Nonetheless, the principle is the same whether in fact or in visualisation: have the feeling of resisting the constricting action of the tight garment.

4. Placement and resonance

The sounds of the human voice are produced in the voice-box (the larynx) and are enhanced by the resonating cavities of the head and throat. These are the nose, the mouth, the back of the mouth (the pharynx) and the windpipe. These structures vary from person to person, and are, to a large degree, responsible for the uniqueness of each human voice. Their size, shape and quality determine the quality (character) of a singer's vocal resonance. The cavities are surrounded by muscles which modify their shape and size, re-configuring them into an infinite number of combined shapes and producing the enormous array of sounds unique to each human individual. This happens each time we speak. As speakers, we rarely or never think about the muscles that control the resonance of the sounds that we make. As singers, we need to be able to produce the sounds that we want. How do we do this without conscious control of each of the dozens of muscles and nerves that are used to produce resonance?

A resonant sound, in singing, is one which has brilliance, colour, intensity and 'ring'. It is sometimes denoted as a singing tone to indicate that the voice is not 'going back into the throat' or 'being swallowed'. It is a sound which 'goes out' into the audience; it 'carries'; it is 'forward'. Notice that all of these descriptions have one thing in common: they are images which connote place. From this effect – which in fact has very little to do with the actual physiology involved in the production of the sound – singers talk about the 'placement' of the voice.

Placement is mental imagery that gives the singer control over the resonance of the sound she is making. Thoughtful, consistent use of this imagery produces a sound that is focused, unconstricted and free of tension. A voice that is correctly supported (see the preceding section) and correctly placed is being used healthily and will develop naturally over a period of time.

The ideal placement of the singing voice is 'forward'. To say this another way: the voice is placed in the facial mask. Singing into the mask (placing the sound forward) will create a buzzing or a feeling of vibration in some part of the front of the face. This sensation may be felt in the lips, the nose, the front teeth or even in the cheekbones. The sensation varies in placement from person to person, but, as long as the vibration is being felt in the mask, the placement is said to be forward. (It is possible, however, to place (feel) the sound far back in the throat, or exclusively in the nose – nasal resonance – or in the back teeth. All these are incorrect.)

To experience the sensation of forward placement, do the following exercise. Pick any note within your range that is comfortable, and hum on 'mmmm', supporting the breath as you have learnt to do in the preceding section, and sustaining the note for a reasonable length of time. Where do you feel the hum? Experiment by singing a higher or a lower pitch to see whether you feel the vibration in a different place in the mask.

To establish and maintain the coordination of the support with consistent forward resonance is an ongoing effort. One of the major tasks of the singer is to keep the sound forward, placing virtually all sounds in the mask. At the same time, the singer must guard against pushing out sound in the mistaken belief that this action assists forward placement. Never try to push the sound out or forward by forcibly tensing the muscles of the abdomen or the throat.

In order to place the sounds of any language correctly, it is necessary to differentiate between vowels and consonants. The vowels in English are a, e, i, o and u. All singing is done on the vowels, while the consonants provide the articulation which distinguishes one word from another. For example, if you sing the vowel 'o' for four beats, the hearer won't be able to recognise the word that you are singing until you end it, for example, with 'ld' or 'dious'. To practise the hum with the vowels, therefore, is to learn how to place the voice for the purpose of singing.

For the humming exercise, practise the hum followed by

the vowels. The usual order and pronunciation are: mee, meh, mah, moh, moo. Take a breath and sing 'mee, meh, mah, moh, moo' in a single breath, *placing each vowel sound in the same place as the hum* (the 'm'), and connecting all the sounds with one another. Choose pitches near the middle of your range when you do this exercise. When you have finished humming on one pitch, take another breath and do the exercise one semi-tone higher. At a certain point, which varies from singer to singer, you will feel that the sound is being constricted, or that the throat is getting tight, or that it is no longer possible to do the hum. At this point, do not continue, but come back down a semi-tone at a time.

Variations:

(a)   Repeat a single hum-vowel over and over on a single breath: 'mee mee mee mee mee'. Make sure that all the sounds are connected, without gaps between them.

(b)   Elongate the hum on the chosen pitch before opening to the vowel: mmmmmmee. Use the hum to establish correct placement before the vowel is attempted.

(c)   Think of the high-pitched whine that a puppy makes when he is asking for attention or a treat. Place the hum at a very high pitch, then glide down on the hum (the 'puppy-dog whine'). Notice how the hum can be felt in various places in the mask. (Every singing teacher has students who refuse point-blank to do this exercise when there is anyone else within earshot. It is useful for several reasons. Firstly, it teaches the sensation of placement in the mask. Secondly, it demonstrates the importance of sound imagery and sound memory in conscious muscle control. Thirdly, the pressure caused by the high-pitched whine causes the lower abdominal muscles to become properly engaged.)

Placement in and beyond the 'passaggio'

Singers who wish to sing the classical repertoire will find that they need to develop the extremities of the vocal range. For these singers, two points are salient. First, a young singer (that is, one in her early to mid teens) must approach both the high and the low extremities of the range with great caution. The voice is not yet mature, and *pushing* the range up or down should be avoided. For these singers, the correct, moderate *exploration* and use of these registers will develop them gradually and healthily. Secondly, the development of these registers, particularly the high register, is generally the work of some years; it cannot be accelerated by forcing the voice or by over-singing.

Passaggio ('pass-adge-jo') is an Italian word meaning 'passage'. Technically speaking, it is the transition between vocal registers that occurs in the normal human voice (section 5). More to the point, the term is used by singers to describe the changes in resonance that occur naturally in the human voice as the singer approaches another register. The term *break* is often used with the same meaning. Many singing teachers avoid this term, since it implies a sudden, rather alarming rupture and may give the false impression that the voice suddenly breaks off or that the transition is sudden. By contrast, the term *passaggio* simply, and more accurately, indicates a transitional area between two natural registers of the voice.

For lower voices, the passaggio occurs in the area of B, C, C♯ that lies above the middle of their range. For higher voices, the passaggio occurs about a third higher: D, E♭, E♮ above the middle of the range. These are only general guidelines. You will know when you have reached the passaggio in your own voice by the sensations (see below).

Ideally, the registers should be joined seamlessly, so that the passaggio between them is no longer obvious. This is achieved through placement. While singing in the passaggio, the singer manipulates the shape of the resonating cavities of the head and throat. This camouflages the transition between the registers so that the sound that emerges is 'seamless' or 'even'; the sound made in the passaggio by a fully trained singer bears no trace of the change of register.

To begin with, sing a major scale starting from the middle of the range that is most comfortable for you. It is likely that this pitch will be around the G above middle C for the soprano and around the E above middle C for the lower female voices. Remember that all voices are different, and that this experiment offers guidelines only: for example, a soprano may be more comfortable beginning on the F♯ above middle C.

Exercise 1

ah - oh -

Sing the scale on a bright 'ah' (as if you were saying 'aha!'), keeping the placement forward, and notice what happens. Normally, as the voice approaches the fifth of the scale (more or less), a constriction or tightness will be felt in the throat. This signals the approach to the passaggio, when the singer often says, 'Oh, I can't sing any higher', or 'That sounds awful, I can't do it.' (I have had many students who can comfortably and reliably sing high C (two octaves above middle C) although they had insisted eighteen months earlier that they would never be able to sing higher than the E a tenth above middle C.)

This will help you to achieve the transition through the passaggio: as soon as you start to feel the constriction in the throat, change the bright 'ah' vowel that you have been singing to the darker 'oh' vowel. *Maintain the same degree and quality of support and, above all, keep the same feeling of placement.*

As you darken to the 'oh' vowel, the throat will open to accommodate the change of vowel. This is perfectly normal. In order to be able to sing high notes and in order to join the registers through the passaggio, you must create more space in the back of the throat. This has the effect of darkening any vowel that is sung on these pitches. To experiment with this, practise opening the throat as if you were going to yawn. The sensation of opening the throat to darken in the passaggio is identical to the sensation that you have at the *beginning* of the yawn. Some teachers talk about the arch at the back of the throat or the cathedral ceiling at the back of the throat. Speaking anatomically, you are lifting the soft palate which normally lies relaxed at the back of the mouth. You can see this if you look closely in the mirror. You are also adjusting the muscles that control the larynx (section 5).

The principle is this: in order to accommodate changes of musculature in the passaggio, you modify the vowel that you sing. In practice, this will mean that a bright vowel (see section 6) will need to be modified whenever it occurs in the passaggio. For example, in the following passage, the bright 'a' of 'glad' will be gradually darkened to a more open sound that approaches an 'o'.

Exercise 2

gla -   -   o -   d

Many singers speak of adding 'oo' or 'oh' to any vowel in the passaggio. This is a different way of saying the same thing. At first, the distortion of the vowel may be so acute that it will be conspicuous. The muscular coordination of the vowel sound with the placement is generally the result of many months or years of work. Approaching the passaggio in this way will:

(a)   open up the voice to make the upper register of the voice accessible;

(b)   eventually smooth out the passaggio to achieve a seamless transition between the middle and upper registers;

(c)   ensure that the voice maintains consistent resonance and brilliance throughout the range (another way of expressing (b) above); and

(d)   eventually establish the placement (the resonance) to the point at which the opening of the throat in the passaggio becomes a natural habit. At this point, the notion of heavily modifying the vowel can be discarded, since the muscles will have been fully re-trained and the muscle memory will enable the muscles to retain the correct position automatically.

Until now, we have discussed only the 'ah' and the 'oh' vowels. Section 6 explains the colouring of all the vowel sounds. First, a brief explanation of the vocal registers is necessary.

5.   The vocal registers

The terminology referring to vocal registers seems confusing (see page 19). The terms low/middle/high, chest/head/ falsetto have been in use for centuries and refer to the sensations of placement that are experienced when these pitches are sung. It is more accurate, however, to think of registers as vocal adjustments to the quality of the tone (the timbre), rather than to its pitch.

Vocal registration is a function of the larynx, or voice-box. Adjustments of the larynx produce different timbres, which we refer to as the registers. When a novice student sings up and down a scale, she will probably notice that her voice has two or even three distinct timbres, depending on whether she is singing 'high' or 'low'. During the act of singing, the larynx creates a pitch by bringing certain muscles into use. As the singer sings a scale and her voice moves into another register, one set of muscles gradually (automatically, natu-rally) takes over from another. The experienced singer has trained these muscles to respond in such a way that the changes in registration are no longer obvious. When this has been achieved, the registers are said to be blended; the change in timbre is no longer obvious. Remember, however, that the adjustments made by the larynx are not abrupt; the areas of transition, as one set of muscles gradually displaces another, is called a passaggio.

The evening out of the vocal registers through the passaggio is achieved through placement (see section 4) and colouring (section 6).

6.   Colour

The terms 'colour', 'tone colour' and 'timbre' are interchangeable. Use of the term 'colour' makes it easy to talk about 'colouring' the voice by darkening the voice, brightening it, adding more 'ee', etc. Deliberately colouring the voice modifies the vocal timbre and contributes to the blending of the registers through conscious adjustments to the vowel and changes to the resonating cavities. Colour is one of the pre-eminent means of expressing the meanings of words. As an example, sing, on a single pitch, the word 'crying' as if you were melancholy. Then sing, on the same pitch, the word 'flying' as if you were deliriously happy. You will, almost certainly, have changed the colour of the vowel sound, although it is the same in each case. Vocal colour is a means of showing or expressing the imaginative content of words. To put it another way, vocal colour is a sensitive response to the imagery inherent in the meaning of the words we sing.

Vocal colour is also amenable to straightforward manipulation of certain muscles, as we have seen in section 4. These exercises aid the joining of the registers by working through the 'ah' to the 'oh' vowel, using the beginning of the yawn to open the back of the throat. But there are three more vowels, plus additional vowel sounds. How should they be sung?

The vowel sounds that are used for vocal exercises are 'ee, eh, ah, oh, oo'. Although the sounds in the following chart have been expressed in terms of English equivalents, they are, in fact, the Italian vowels, which are pure; that is, unlike English vowels, they do not contain dipthongs. Furthermore, the natural placement of the Italian vowels is in the mask. These should be pronounced like the vowels in the following words:

ee like the ee in free (Italian 'i' as in Italia)

eh like the a in dare (Italian 'e' as in amore)

ah like the a in man (Italian 'a' as in amore)

oh like the o in go (Italian 'o' as in altro)

oo like the o in do (Italian 'u' as in luna).

Note: when singing 'ah' be careful not to allow it to drop into the dead vowel 'uh' (as in 'cut'). In the lower register, make sure that the vowel is a bright 'ah' sound (as in 'man'); do not darken it to the 'aw' sound of 'awe'.

When a singer is using the register which lies below the passaggio, in the lower or middle part of the voice, the vowels will retain, more or less, the purity of the Italian vowels. This is generally true regardless of the language in which she is singing. For pop and rock music, and for some musical theatre, these vowel sounds are often used throughout the range, even when the range is extended to include notes in the passaggio and beyond. That is, frequently, the blending of the registers is unimportant in these types of music, and the lack of blending is considered acceptable or even desirable.

For the singer who wishes to perform classical music, however, and for most musical theatre, the registers must be blended, as we have seen. To do this, we have started below the passaggio with the pure, bright vowel sound 'ah' (Italian 'a') and darkened it in the passaggio into the pure, dark vowel 'oh' (Italian 'o'). To achieve this, we have opened the back of the throat, as if beginning to yawn. This action has changed the colour of the vowel.

I reiterate these points because this is, conceptually, the most difficult aspect of vocal technique. In order to blend the registers, it is necessary to darken all the vowels in the passaggio by opening the back of the throat as if beginning to yawn. The pure vowels which you have been singing below the passaggio are going to be darkened in order to adjust to the natural (involuntary) changes in the musculature of the larynx and to give, thereby, *the illusion that you are not making changes*. Darken by (1) creating the sensation of the beginning of the yawn at the back of the throat, while (2) maintaining the forward placement. (Do not allow the sound to 'go back'.) At this stage, the vowels will no longer be pure, but the voice is being correctly produced. With continued practice in this way, the muscles will be re-trained to produce a seamless registration in which the placement is forward. The vowels will gradually regain their clarity.

To see how this works, try this exercise.

Exercise 3

ee - - ö -

To produce this sound, sing 'e' as in 'pet', but point the lips.

Check the position of the mouth by looking in the mirror. Keep the mouth open, dropping the jaw and allowing it to relax. Any tension of the jaw or throat must be avoided. In the passaggio, some students have the tendency to draw the lips in, pressing them in against the teeth. Instead, point the lips slightly outward, bringing them forward away from the teeth. Do not, however, hold them in a rigid position. Holding the lips away from the teeth helps to relax the muscles of the jaw, as well as to bring the sound forward. Experiment by singing a free, open 'oh' in the passaggio with the lips pointing forward. Then, while continuing the 'oh', change the position of the lips, drawing them in to the teeth. The differences will be conspicuous.

It will have become obvious that the requisite ease and dexterity for these technical changes develops only over a period of time. Think of the rider whose leg muscles and ligaments are re-trained to spiral around the horse's side in order to keep the heel down and to apply the leg aids properly. Think of the yoga master who has spent long hours training the muscles of his legs to accommodate comfortably to the lotus position. This will give some idea of the re-training that is involved in blending the registers.

Remember that the exaggerated distortion of the vowels that you may hear when you first do these exercises is a means to an end. Persevere and you will gradually retrain the muscles to adopt new positions that will enable you to sing freely and clearly, without an obvious break between registers.

7. Phrasing

Music is thought of in terms of phrases. Music, we say, is divided into phrases for technical or artistic purposes. A phrase is meant to be sung in one breath. All this is true. Nonetheless, this explanation is rather like saying that we consciously divide our speech into sentences because our purpose in speaking is to use grammar correctly. Our healthy and coordinated breathing technique will help us to sing phrases correctly, but our ultimate goal is to use our technique to make beautiful and expressive music.

Phrasing involves much more than demonstrating an ability to sing phrases in one breath. Take as an example the following:

Exercise 4

To   mur - mur   at   last,___   a - las,   a - las.

If the composer or editor of a piece of music does not indicate the phrasing, the singer (or her accompanist or teacher) must decide where to breathe. The tendency of novice singers is to take two breaths in this line, since the rests indicate two breaks in the sound. Breathing before each 'alas' divides the line into three phrases. This creates a choppy effect which seems to run counter to the poet's intentions. The text, the mood, the minor key, the echoing assonance and consonance of the words 'at last, alas, alas', the low tessitura, all seem to indicate that the singer should be striving to murmur the words quietly, without disturbing the surface of the sound.

A musical phrase is a complete thought. If possible, musical and poetic considerations should carry more weight in determining phrasing than technical ones.

Most singers phrase in the following manner, singing the phrase in one breath, merely stopping the sound ('lifting') after 'at last' and 'alas'.

Exercise 5

This preserves the sense of regret or resignation implicit in the poetry. Poetry has its own music to which the singer should be sensitive. Musical phrasing is the art of using the breath to express the thought.

Legato

Legato is essential to the development of good vocal technique and to musical phrasing. This Italian word, meaning 'smooth' or 'connected', is used by all musicians to indicate a seamless connection between sounds. Some instruments, such as the drum or the harpsichord, are not capable of producing a true legato. Most instruments, however, including the human voice, possess the acoustical apparatus that enables them to produce a true legato line.

Unless the music or the exercise specifies otherwise, all music should be sung legato; that is, all the sounds should be connected smoothly. Involuntary breaks in the legato sound should not be caused by:

(a)   Changing from one vowel sound to another.

(b)   Changing from a vowel to a consonant or vice versa.

(c)   Changing from one pitch to another.

(d)   Moving from one register to another.

Section 4 (Placement and resonance) states that all singing is done on the vowels but that it is the consonants that make the words recognisable. How is true legato (smooth, connected singing) possible if the vowel sounds are constantly being interrupted by consonants, which break up the sound? To maintain a legato line while singing words, it is necessary to move very quickly from vowel to vowel, passing through the consonant without allowing it to affect the sound of either vowel. It helps to think of each syllable as beginning with a consonant and ending with a vowel.

To try this, choose a line (one that contains several words) of any song you are familiar with. Sing the line through using only the vowel sounds; then sing it again, this time singing the words and consciously using the vowel sounds to keep legato flowing. Take, for example, the line 'God save our gracious Queen'. Singing on the vowels, the line becomes 'oh eh ah-oo eh uh ee'. Now, take a song you know and try singing it using only the vowels.

Practising any song by singing the vowels alone will help you to work it into the muscles and to sing it smoothly. If you have a vocal line which is marked 'staccato' (each note separated from the others), practise singing the vowels legato first, then staccato. The staccato will be much easier to sing in tune.

A legato musical phrase consists of a line of smoothly connected vowel sound(s) articulated by consonants which do not interrupt that legato. It helps to imagine the legato musical phrase as a stream of flowing water (the sound) into which you drop a leaf (a consonant) without interrupting the flow of the stream.

To establish the sensation of legato in the muscles, the following exercises are useful.

Exercise 6

ah   -   -   -

Exercise 7

ah   -   -   -

Exercise 8

ah   -   o   - ah   -

The glissando (slur, portamento) is a useful aid in establishing a reliable legato sound. This term is used frequently in string music. It is indicated like this:

Exercise 9

When a string player sees this indication, she plays all the pitches between the first and last pitch by sliding her finger over the sounding string. Although the voice is produced by a mechanism that is completely different from that of the stringed instruments, the same glissando can be used in exercises to help develop a true legato line.

It is also helpful to use the glissando when the line of a song moves in and out of the passaggio. Under these circumstances, the placement sometimes tends to go askew, causing the vocal line to break up. The glissando enables the singer to feel and establish the correct placement throughout the line. After using the glissando in a particular piece for practice purposes, however, discontinue its use. It is almost never used by singers in performance.

Exercise 10

Lento

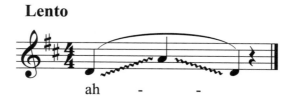

ah -   -

Practise this slowly; slide from one note to another, but stop at each note to establish the correct pitch before you go on to the next glissando. Exaggerate the slide in order to maintain consistent placement of the sound. Maintain the awareness of the sensation. After you have worked the sensation of the placement into your voice, discard the glissando.

Flexibility

Vocal flexibility can be achieved only when the singer has gained adequate control of the elements of technique discussed in the preceding sections of this chapter. It can be defined as the ability to sing rapid passages in tune, using a free and correct tone, phrasing, placement and breath control. This exercise is an example of such a passage:

Exercise 11

When the singer is capable of tackling such music, she will find exercises which challenge and develop this ability. Many singers use passages of florid music from the operas of Mozart, Handel, Donizetti, Bellini and others as exercises. The rapid changes from note to note that characterise such music must be produced *from the diaphragm (from the abdominal support) and not from the larynx (the voice-box)*.

The exercises are given in order of progressive difficulty.

Exercise 12

Exercise 13

Exercise 14

ah - - oh - - ah -

8. The practice session

One of the greatest operatic singers of the twentieth-century, the Wagnerian soprano Birgit Nilsson, relates an anecdote about her own practice sessions. She was warming up for a performance in her dressing room when she was interrupted by a policeman who had heard her from the alleyway outside and came into the building through the stage door, demanding to know what was going on. When he was told that the singer was warming up for a concert, he was astonished. As far as he was concerned, he said, the woman sounded like an elephant that had had its foot stamped on. Miss Nilsson, with characteristic candour and good humour, admitted that, to most people, the sounds of warming up don't sound very musical, or even pleasant.

The practice session is a period of time dedicated to work on vocal technique and, possibly but not always, to work on the music that is being studied. It is not a rehearsal or a mock performance designed to impress an audience. It is generally done in private, and it may not sound very pleasant to an outsider, since the singer is constantly building a skill at which no one ever becomes perfect. Singers must guard against being put off by nay-sayers like Miss Nilsson's policeman! When she was a singing student in Sweden, she was told more than once that a farmer's daughter had no business trying to learn how to sing grand opera. She never allowed herself to become discouraged by the prejudices and narrow-mindedness of others. Like her, all singers must strive to maintain a positive attitude.

The following story describes an ideal practice session, and can be used as a model for your own practice. The most important elements of the session are in italics. The character, Sarah, is a soprano who has been studying singing for about eight months. As you read the story, it will help if you visualise yourself as Sarah. Change the scene as you wish. Instead of the full-length mirror beside the piano, you might have a mirror in the hallway. If you don't have a piano, an inexpensive electronic keyboard or a pitchpipe will do just as well. And, of course, you may wish to change the character from Sarah to David. Just visualise yourself in a relaxed, pleasant setting as you 'walk through' this practice session.

Sarah *closed the door* behind her and walked over to the full-length *mirror* that hung on the wall beside the piano. Closing her eyes, she took a couple of deep breaths through her nose, and felt the breath settling itself each time deeply in her abdomen. Sarah felt her rib cage expand and her abdomen push out. The *slow, centred breathing* filled her with a sense of relaxation. She took a few more breaths through her nose, but this time, as she exhaled, she allowed the air to spin out through her pursed lips and *as she consciously established the sensation of support*. Sarah opened her eyes. Each time she exhaled through pursed lips, she could feel the *resistance* in her body as the chest and abdomen maintained the air pressure that had been created when she took in the breath. Stretching her arms overhead to the ceiling as she inhaled and looked up, she allowed the stretch to open and lengthen her body. As she exhaled, she brought her arms down to her sides and checked her posture in the mirror. She felt *centred and full of energy*.

Sarah always *used a couple of variations on the humming exercise to start her warm-up*. She went over to the piano and *stood* in front of the keyboard. She struck the F above middle C and re-established her posture before beginning to sing. She started on the F and sang 'mee, meh, mah, moh, moo', *using the hum to place the sound in the mask*. Then she struck the F♯ and stood tall again, repeating the exercise. Sarah followed the same procedure to hum up to the D a sixth higher than her starting pitch. Then she came back down, a semi-tone at a time, until she reached middle C. *After a couple of minutes of humming, she felt warmed up enough to start stretching the voice a bit further,* and she did this by singing a series of scales. She started on middle C on 'ah' and sang the scale both up and down. Then she did the same starting on C♯. When she got to the D she sang on 'ah' as far as the upper C♯, and then she darkened the last note, the D, to 'oh' before coming back down again on 'ah'. She was *careful to make sure her throat was open on the D as if she were starting to yawn.* She struck the lower D♯ on the piano. Starting on 'ah' and going up by semi-tones, Sarah darkened the D and the D♯ when she reached the upper octave. She wasn't really satisfied that the placement was as forward as she would have liked, but she had noticed a lot of improvement in the last month, and she *persevered* day by day. Sarah carried the exercise all the way up to the G, darkening each note that lay in the passaggio.

The voice felt much warmer and more responsive by now. Sarah wanted to work on the flexibility of her voice and she *started with an exercise that used a fairly small range.* She *continued with a more difficult one that stretched her range and challenged her to use all of the energy and support she could muster.* Each time she practised, she became *more aware* of the growing coordination of the breath support with the placement.

By this time it was *about twenty minutes into the practice session,* and Sarah felt warmed up enough to start working on her music. She was learning a song by Schubert. She had bought the sheet music and picked out the tune on the piano. She had also bought a CD so that she could listen to it over and over. This had helped her to *learn the notes,* but she didn't always feel confident that she could consistently sing the notes – place the notes – precisely where she wanted them. Listening to the music and *practising it in different ways* over the past couple of days had really helped with this.

Sarah placed the sheet music on her music stand and *adjusted the height so that she could stand tall and see the music without having to bend her head.* She started by singing the whole piece through, *resisting the temptation to bend over and play the notes on the piano as she sang.* Then she started to work on the piece. First, she *hummed the entire piece through.* Next, Sarah *sang through the whole piece on the vowels,* using her knowledge of *placement to keep the sound forward.* There were a couple of phrases that she wasn't happy with, so she stopped and *worked through them* until she felt that they were well supported and more forward. Finally, she *added the consonants.* She concentrated on *creating a smooth legato line,* singing on the vowels and just *using the consonants for articulation without disturbing the legato.*

A couple of the phrases were quite taxing in terms of breath control. What had seemed fairly easy when she was just singing the vowels became much more difficult when she added the consonants. She *experimented* with more support and different dynamic levels (volume of sound) until she found something that seemed to work. In *thinking through the apparent difficulty,* she realised that the phrasing depended on the preparation for the breath and the support. She reminded herself that *things don't happen overnight,* and that coordinating the breath with the support is an ongoing task for every singer.

Working on the music in this way had taken another *twenty minutes or so.* Sarah was starting to feel tired, but there was another piece she had been working on for some time and she wanted to sing through it a couple of times before stopping for the day.

'Maybe I'd better *have a break* before I go on,' she said to herself. She made herself a cup of tea and carried it back with her to the practice room. The notebook that she had bought to jot down ideas and queries – *a sort of progress report for herself* – lay open on the table beside the piano. She sat down with it and made a few notes about today's session while she drank her tea.

The other piece was a folk-song arrangement that she had worked on a few months ago. Refreshed by the tea, Sarah sang through the song using only the vowels, and when she sang through it again using the words, she was pleased to feel how easy it had become. The phrases that she had worked so hard on had actually *worked themselves into the voice during those daily practice sessions.* Sarah had a sense that the music was singing itself, that her *muscles remembered* what she had trained them to do.

She had tried to explain the feeling to her friend Lisa a couple of weeks ago, when she had experienced the same feeling with another song. 'It's like putting yourself on automatic,' she said. 'The work has all been done – and believe me, it *is* work – but when you have the feeling of *owning the music* – I mean that it's yours, your own interpretation that you sing in your own unique voice – well, nothing beats it. When you get to that stage, you just feel as though the music is coming out in a natural flow, and you can enjoy the feeling for its own sake. You have a sense of release and freedom and a real buzz. Fantastic.'

Sarah realised it was time to finish for the day. She had read that it was important to *finish the practice session by doing something that left her with a sense of success.* Putting this into practice had helped her to get through some rough times when nothing – or nearly nothing – seemed to be going right. She made a last note in her singing diary: 'Sang through "Down by the Salley Gardens". Would make *a great party piece* – it's MY PIECE!'

9. Vocal strain

Abuse of the voice will eventually result in damage to the vocal apparatus. This damage may take the form of irritation manifesting itself in persistent sore throat or hoarseness. This in turn may cause total or partial laryngitis (inflammation of the larynx). It is sometimes difficult to track down the source of such problems, since they are associated with the common cold as well as with vocal strain.

More serious damage can take the form of nodes (tumours caused by friction between the vocal ligaments), polyps (tumours on the mucous membrane of the vocal cords) or contact ulcers. For the singer afflicted with one of these serious problems, medical attention is necessary. Surgery and a long period of vocal rest may be required.

To help avoid these conditions, take the following precautions:

- Avoid over-tiring the voice. Singing for hours on end, unless you are a professional who is 'marking' during rehearsals, is an invitation to vocal trouble. Young singers, whose voices are not fully mature, need to be especially careful.

- Do not sing under the following conditions: if you are physically very tired; in the open air, especially if it is cold; in dusty environments.

- Avoid well-meant advice that has no basis in fact.

- If you are in your teens, be careful not to strain the voice if you are singing in a group of older singers with mature voices. Soprano and tenor voices, in particular, can sustain damage by singing too high, too heavily or too loudly.

- If you have a cold, it is usually all right to sing unless you are tired or have a sore throat. A sore throat is a warning that tells you to stop singing.

- Singing should not cause a sore throat. If you often find yourself with a sore throat after singing, you should stop singing and seek the advice of a reputable singing teacher. The solution may be straightforward and the problem easy to correct.

- Be sensible in your practice. If you are used to singing for a few minutes each day while you are in the car going to work, or while you are doing your homework, don't start out by devoting two hours each day to practice. If you are just beginning to study singing, start by practising for twenty minutes or half an hour five days a week. In a month's time, add ten or fifteen minutes to your practice time, and so on. (See section 8.) You are building muscle strength and muscle tone, as well as coordination.

10. Style

In general, a solid vocal technique is the basis of any healthy, trouble-free singing, whether you sing classical, rock or show music. Singers who sing the classical repertoire are expected to have 'big' voices; that is, they have to be able to project their voices into a very large auditorium without using a microphone. They are also expected to have a very large range with no discernible 'breaks' of registration. In order to keep their voices healthy and performing well under such demanding conditions, they must have an excellent vocal technique. Vocal technique is defined as a coherent *method of singing* that is based on the knowledgeable, healthy and purposive use of the human voice. The skill can be learned by anyone who puts in the requisite time and effort.

Vocal style is genre-specific *performance practice*. For example, hip-hop and blues demand different styles of singing. Having said that, it is possible to sing *Caro mio ben* (an eighteenth-century art song) in a blues style, or *Yesterday* in an operatic style. A few songs, such as *Summertime*, from Gershwin's *Porgy and Bess* can work in a variety of vocal styles. Today, a singer with a solid vocal technique is not confined to only one genre, and can easily sing in several different vocal styles. Singers like Cleo Laine, Placido Domingo and Lesley Garrett demonstrate again and again that good technique is transferrable from one style to another.

Chapter 5:

Musical Skills

Knowing a song

What does it mean to 'know' a song? Two friends were listening to a piece of music on the radio. One was a professional musician, and the other was self-confessedly unmusical. The non-musical friend asked the musician, 'Do you know this music?' Without thinking, the musician replied that she knew the choral version (which she had sung some years before) but not the orchestral version (the one being played). Her friend gave her a strange look but said nothing. When the piece finished, the announcer gave the name of the work and the composer. The friend triumphantly exclaimed, 'Oh, so that's what it was!' Her question had meant, 'Can you identify that piece of music?' To the musician, the question had meant, 'Do you know this music well enough to perform it?', and she had answered accordingly.

If a young singing pupil – a beginner – is asked to learn a song on her own, she will probably come to her next lesson having played through the melody a couple of times on the piano. She is not necessarily being careless or indifferent. From her point of view, she has learnt the song. The tune and the words are vaguely familiar to her. If the song were played on the radio, she would recognise it as the one she has learnt.

Clearly, the concept of knowing or learning a song can mean different things to different people. But for the singer to be able to claim that she knows, or has learnt, a piece of music, she must be able to do more than merely identify or recognise it. She must be ready to perform it with a certain degree of mastery and conviction. This chapter describes the process of getting a piece of music to that stage.

Like other musicians, singers have certain resources at their disposal which they can use to learn music. The musical score, with its markings and instructions, is one such tool. Other helps are a systematic approach, a keyboard (not always necessary), performances on CD, vocal technique, and, last but not least, that most wonderful resource, the accompanist. Not all singers have access to all of these aids, but most manage to find what they need.

The musical score

To someone who does not read music, the musical score can seem a meaningless set of scratches on the paper. Yet, with a little effort it can be made intelligible. Classes on score-reading, sight-singing or music-reading are sometimes offered as part of community programmes or as non-credit extension courses at universities. Courses are also available on the Internet, and many books have been written on the subject. These have the advantage of being readily accessible when you have time to use them, and they can be used as reference material or an adjunct to the fun of learning in a group.

Musical scores can come in many editions, versions and arrangements:

1.   Melody only.

2.   Piano/vocal score. This has the voice part on one line, and the piano part on two lines below it.

3.   SATB version, a choral arrangement. It may or may not include a piano accompaniment.

4.   Orchestral version. This may be a full score or a miniature score. It contains all the instrumental parts, of which the voice part is just one.

For solo singing, use the piano/vocal score. This may be sheet music, consisting of only the song you want. If the song is from a musical or opera, you may want the full piano/vocal score, which contains all the music in the entire work. Choral arrangements should not be substituted for the piano/vocal score or vice versa; it is important to buy the correct version. An authentic edition of the work should be used unless your teacher or musical director specifies another. In poor editions, operatic arias may be in the wrong key; arrangements may be inaccurate or poorly constructed; songs in foreign languages may be badly translated or the original words may be omitted or incorrectly transcribed.

Score-reading for singers

A musical score contains an enormous amount of information. Some of it is written in musical notation, some in words, and some in symbols. Whether or not you read music at this stage, it would be wise to buy a dictionary of musical terms. It explains the verbal indications – such as tempo markings – in detail, and gives examples. The dictionary will also explain the symbols that are in common use, such as dynamic markings. ('Dynamics' are indications of relative loudness and softness.) A good dictionary is a small investment to make, and will pay for itself many times over in terms of the confidence and knowledge that you gain from using it whenever you approach a song.

Experienced musicians always mark their scores. Some musicians add so many indications to their scores that they become almost unreadable by anyone else who looks at them. The important point, however, is that the musician makes her score into an individually personalised 'road map' to assist her in performing the music. The marks that she makes will not only help her to sing the music without error; they will remind her of actions she must take to avoid technical pitfalls.

Where scores are on loan from a library, a singer should be aware that any marks made will need to be removed before the copies are returned, so be sure to use a soft pencil. However, when a choral singer purchases her own music it would be hugely beneficial to go through the entire score and highlight with a transparent coloured highlighter pen the text that she has to sing. This will help prevent the eyes from leaping to the wrong line of music when reading along. Both choral and solo singers could circle changes of tempo or key. Awkward entrances might be announced with a star or a pair of spectacles drawn above the musical line to indicate, 'Attention here!'

Certain conventions that occur only in vocal music can trap even musicians who read music and can play other instruments. In all music, the slur is a curved line that is used to show that two consecutive notes are to be played in a connected (legato) fashion. In vocal music, however, it indicates this and more. The slur means that the syllable of text which is written beneath the first note of the slur is to be carried over into the following note or notes. For example:

Exercise 15

all   my   long - ing

Approaching the music

Depending on how well you read music, learning a new piece can be a step-by-step approach as outlined below. If you are already an experienced singer, you will find that many of these steps actually take place concurrently. Learning a piece and getting it into shape is ideally an organic, rather than a linear, process. Start by looking at the title. It probably conveys quite a lot about the song, but it is remarkable how few singers bother about it.

1.   LEARNING THE NOTES

Many people are tempted to learn music by singing along with a CD. There is some evidence that singing along with videos, CDs or with other people is beneficial to the novice or younger singer. It inspires confidence, discourages self-consciousness ('listening to yourself') and, in general, helps to give a sense of freedom and naturalness to the act of singing. And, as you are aware, it can help you learn the music. If, however, you are interested in producing your own interpretation of a song rather than in imitating someone else's, you should go to the original score and look at the composer's own markings for tempo, dynamics and other musical considerations. In addition to this, it is difficult, while you're imitating the style of someone else's singing, not to imitate her voice as well. Her voice may be nothing like yours.

Playing the notes on a piano will also help you to learn them, in the initial stages, as something external to yourself, but to know a piece of music means that you have worked it into your voice. In the same way that your golf swing or your ability to ski moguls or to mimic the prime minister (or any physical skill that you have mastered) is part of your intuitive muscle knowledge and your muscle memory, knowing a piece of music means that you have worked it into your muscle memory by practising it accurately.

A melody is a series of related notes, which have a certain length and a certain pitch, and rests (silences) which have a certain length. To learn the notes means that you learn the correct notes, in rhythm, along with the rests. In practice, this means learning the notes and the rests in relation to each other.

The best way to do this is to look carefully at the music first. You'll notice certain things at this early stage which can help you later. Try to get a feel for the shape of the melody and where it lies in your voice. Does it lie very high, or very low, in your voice? Is it in a major or a minor key? What is the range of the piece – what are the highest and the lowest notes? Are certain phrases too long to handle in one breath? Where will you breathe? Are certain phrases, or sections, repeated, perhaps on different words? Is the song strophic (that is, does it contain several verses of poetry, each one using the same melody)? Or is it 'through-composed' – does each stanza or section have new music? Are there any parts which look more complicated? Does the key of the piece change? The tempo? The key signature? (These are all worth marking with a pencil.) Are there parts which are highly chromatic? Which are florid? Look at the accompaniment, too, or the other parts, if it is a choral piece. Does the introduction contain the same melody as the vocal line? How will you get your opening pitch? Is it given to you in the piano part? Or do you start singing before the piano part comes in? If there is a long interlude when you do not sing, how will you know when to come in again, and on what pitch? Look at the words, too. If it is in a language which you know, or if there is a translation, what do the words convey? What is the mood of the piece? Do the words, the accompaniment and the melody seem to go together? Do they all seem to convey the same emotional idea?

Now select a single, comfortable vowel, such as 'ah'. Sing through the music on this vowel, using a keyboard if it helps, without paying too much attention to the tempo or the rests. Don't forget your technique just because you are 'merely' learning the notes. Try to sing out, and don't sit at the piano if you can possibly avoid it – it is too easy to scrunch over and forget to support the voice! Are there some pitfalls that you did not notice when you were first looking through the piece? Notice the intervals – the movement between the notes: is it generally stepwise, or are there large leaps? Do the leaps bridge the registers of your voice? If so, how will you handle this?

As you work through this stage of the learning process, aim for three things: learn the notes, keep the production of the voice free, sing legato. Your purpose is to work the piece into your voice, guiding your muscles to accommodate to the shape and nuance of the melody. You are aiming to express the vocal line in as beautiful a way as you can, right from the start. Even if there are sections marked 'staccato', sing them legato for now, because the vocal line always depends on the mental ideal of legato.

This may seem like a time-consuming process. In fact, approaching the music in this way will save you time in the long term and will build good learning habits. As you become used to learning music in this way, many of these steps become automatic.

2.   LEARNING THE MUSIC

Now read the words as text, going away from the music. If the song is in a foreign language, make sure that you have a good grasp of the words. To understand the text means to know what each of the words means – nouns, verbs, adjectives and adverbs – and to know how they function in context. In the poetry of any language, normal word order is often inverted. The grammar and syntax of other languages follow different rules from those of English. The interpretation of poetry, even in one's native language, is not straightforward. Always make sure, by any means you can, that you know the meaning of the text that you are singing.

Now go back to the music and just look at the note lengths, the rests and the editorial markings, including dynamics. How do these support the meaning of the poetry? For example, do the vocal part and the accompaniment get louder to indicate frustration, quieter to indicate calm resignation?

You also by now have developed a feel for the shape of the melody, so it's time to make music. Instead of singing the notes on 'ah', sing the notes on the vowels of the words while you still maintain the fluid movement of the legato. For example, the words 'he loves me' will no longer be sung 'ah ah ah', but 'ee uh ee'. Notice what happens to the 'feel' of the vocal line when you add the vowels. At this point, notice again tied notes, slurs and repeated notes. Do the vowels have an effect on the emotional content of the line? Are any of the vowel sounds awkward to sing because of where they lie in the voice?

3.   MAKING IT YOUR OWN

You have by now learnt the notes, you understand the poetry, you have incorporated some of the dynamics and phrasing into your singing, and you can now 'fine-tune' your interpretation. Now, get rid of the notes. Choose one pitch that is comfortable for you to sing, in the middle of your range, and sing the text, in rhythm, on that one pitch.

Put the whole thing together.

To learn the music, you have explored the potential of each aspect, first in isolation and then in combination with the others.

Different kinds of songs

Individual songs and song cycles

A song is usually a single musical piece for solo voice or for several voices, written with or without accompaniment. A song cycle is a set of songs related by means of textual and (often) musical theme. The best songs in any language use texts of outstanding poetic quality, and the music of both the singer and the accompanist or orchestra adds another dimension of expression to the text in the same way that the quality of an actor's voice conveys the meaning of the text he is speaking. In songs, the meaning and the sound of the words become interwoven. Each singer's interpretation will be different, and each performance will be different. The depth of the interpretation will increase with each performance.

Songs or arias that are part of a larger work

If the song or aria is part of a show, an oratorio or an opera, you should become familiar with the whole score, and particularly with the character whose music you are singing. These are primarily dramatic – that is, they tell stories. Whether or not they are staged, they are usually presented with their full, original orchestral accompaniment, although amateur or semi-professional companies may produce them using a piano reduction of the whole score. Individual arias, presented as part of a recital programme or an audition, are usually accompanied by piano. The texts of operas are not

always of a very high poetic quality, although many exceptions to this generalisation exist. There are two kinds of arias.

- Recitative and aria. These are found in most operas,
  oratorios and musicals. The recitative is normally part
  of the narrative. It *tells* what is happening or it *describes*
  how the character is reacting to something that has
  happened, or is about to happen. It is followed by the
  aria, which *shows* how the character is feeling because of
  what has happened. The audience needs to grasp the
  textual information contained in the recitative, so the
  words must be sung distinctly. In the aria, the emotional impact of the words and music is paramount.
  This does not give the singer permission to let herself
  get carried away by the emotion of the piece. On the
  contrary, in order to express the emotion that the character is feeling, the singer must sing technically. In this
  way she will be able to communicate the character's
  emotion to the audience.

- Da capo aria. An aria may be in da capo ('from the head,
  from the top') form: the first section (A) is repeated
  after the second section (B), hence A-B-A. In the seven-
  teenth and eighteenth centuries, the repeated A section
  was ornamented; that is, the melody was made more
  elaborate.

Working on a role

Singing an entire role in an opera or musical places demands
on your physical and vocal stamina, your time, your technique and your memory.

- Learn the individual parts of the music in the way I have
  outlined above. Do not neglect the ensembles, the spoken parts, the parts that seem like so much wordy
  connective tissue, in favour of the big arias. Many inexperienced performers think that the small, 'unimportant' bits will take care of themselves and 'come

together' during rehearsals. Never count on this. Never leave anything to chance. Never neglect any part of the role.

- Listen to every CD, watch every video, go to every performance, that you can, not only of the work which you will be performing, but of other works by the same composer or by other composers in the same genre.

- Analyse each. What worked and what didn't? What did you like or not like?

- You will normally be given help in learning the role by a rehearsal accompanist, coach or répétiteur. Take full advantage of the invaluable services that these people offer. They love singing as much as you do, and will share their insight into the role you're studying. Never underestimate the part they play in your success or take them for granted.

- Coach the role with your own accompanist.

- Use your time wisely. Write out a schedule of practice, rehearsals and deadlines for learning certain sections of the work. Break the role down into smaller chunks so that you don't end up feeling overwhelmed.

- Above all, begin work now.

- Take regular breaks. Don't oversing.

- In rehearsals, there is nothing wrong with 'marking'. This means singing your music in half-voice and singing the high notes an octave lower than written. Save your voice. You're not indestructible.

- Do some research on the work. Operas are often based on plays, novels or legends. They frequently have political or cultural overtones relating to the time and place in which they were written. Oratorios are usually based upon Biblical texts, either in Latin or in the vernacular. Musicals can be based upon poetic texts, stories or the life of a real person. All works of music have a 'performance history'. What was the initial reaction to the first performance? Who sang in the original production? Did the composer write several versions? Was it more popular in one country than in another? Knowing the origins and history of the work should be part of your study.

When the music has been learnt

Music that is learnt in this way becomes part of the muscle memory and the neural network of the singer and will probably stay with her for the rest of her life. Most singers, both professional and non-professional, can tell stories of hearing a song, or of being asked to perform a song, that they used to sing but have not looked at or even thought about, for many years. They are surprised when the song returns to them in a state even fresher, more secure and more spontaneous than when they had first learnt it.

Chapter 6:

Training the Voice

At some stage, virtually all singers think about training their voices – 'taking singing lessons'. This chapter discusses ways of assessing whether singing lessons would be beneficial, how to find a teacher and alternatives to formal singing lessons. Interwoven with information and suggestions is another thread, that of expectation. At each level of considering and decision-making, there is a question that the prospective student needs to ask: what are my expectations – of myself, of my teacher and of our work together?

Who can benefit from taking singing lessons?

It is not necessarily the people with the 'best' singing voices who benefit the most from taking singing lessons. There are many, many people with excellent singing voices who sing for the pure pleasure of it, but who lack the time, interest or commitment to take their hobby a step further either by reading books about it or by looking for a singing teacher. Misguided friends or teachers badger these singers by repeated suggestions that they take singing lessons, since they 'have such a gift, it would be a shame not to do something with it'. They may go to a teacher, discover that voice training is not just a matter of 'getting a few tips', and stop after only a few lessons with a feeling of discouragement or disappointment in themselves or in 'the system'. They would have been much better off just continuing as they were; that is, by whole-heartedly enjoying their singing.

Others may feel that they do not have voices that are 'good

enough'. They may sing in a church or community choir, or in the shower, and they're always eager to listen to singing, either live or on CD. They attend as many concerts and performances as they can. They've always been interested in singing, but have always felt that they couldn't justify the expense of singing lessons. They may even feel that no singing teacher would be willing to take them on. Yet it is this group of singers to whom voice training could be of real benefit.

Why is this so? Because the motivation that lies behind the desire to take singing lessons has to come from within the person, and it has to be rather strong, in order to carry the singer through the ups and downs of voice training. What the untrained singer perceives as her potential or as the 'inherent quality' of her voice carries much less weight in determining the final outcome of the lessons, than her motivation.

Of what, exactly, does a singing lesson consist?

A singing lesson is usually a half-hour to an hour-long session. Generally, the lesson consists of the singing student and her voice teacher, although an accompanist may participate in part of the session. Singing lessons are sometimes shared with another student. In this case, the students may sing together for at least part of the time, but the teacher should listen to each individually as well. Two novice students sharing a lesson, if they are well-matched, have the opportunity to learn from each other's experiences.

The singing lesson generally consists of three sections: a warm-up, work on vocal technique and work on specific music. This schedule is flexible, however. Warming up exercises usually serve specific technical purposes, and work on the music is usually approached from the technical angle as well as from the interpretive side. Work on technique may be sacrificed from time to time if the student and the teacher agree, in order to work on music, perhaps if the former is preparing for a recital or an audition, etc. The warm-up should never be omitted, although it may be feasible for an advanced student to come to the lesson 'already warmed up'. In any case, the emphasis during the lesson is on vocal technique; that is, on how to sing correctly and healthily, and to develop the student's potential.

How to find a singing teacher

Some singing teachers specialise in certain styles of music such as jazz, pop, rock, heavy metal or hip-hop. Classically trained singing teachers do not usually specialise in any particular type of music. Although the technique that they teach is usually applied to 'classical' or 'serious' music, it can, in fact, be used to sing any kind of music. It is the responsibility of any singing teacher to teach the student a healthy, correct and consistent singing technique regardless of the genre or style of music to which it is going to be applied.

Whether the student is looking for a teacher of a particular style or for a teacher of classical technique, she will probably not have much difficulty in finding one who suits her needs. She can go to concerts, recitals, competitions and music festivals and ask the competitors and performers. If there is a local or up-and-coming young singer whom the prospective student admires, she could approach her and ask her for information. If there is a local music school or university where singing is taught as an academic subject, the singing teacher may accept private students. At universities or schools of music, advanced or postgraduate singing students may take beginners. Choral conductors sometimes know of local singing teachers. Finally, some teachers advertise in local and national publications and even on the Internet.

What makes a good singing teacher?

A singing teacher will help the student to recognise and reach her potential as a singer by developing her voice.

It is important that you feel comfortable and at ease with the teacher. Any of the professional teachers and coaches with whom you work should have your best long-term interests in mind.

A good singing teacher knows how to sing, has a thorough understanding of vocal technique, and can communicate this information in a timely and appropriate fashion to her students. She also communicates her love and enthusiasm for singing to her students. A lesson is always exciting. It is a quest for the best in the student.

A prospective teacher may have credentials in the fields of singing (performance or teaching). While possession of such a degree from a recognised institution will give you some indication of training, the lack of such a degree is not necessarily a drawback or an indication of lack of ability. Many fine professional singers have no formal qualifications. If they teach, they may or may not be able to communicate their knowledge effectively, or they may sing instinctively and have no real understanding of how they produce their sound. Even if this is the case, however, you may be 'on the same wave length', and find that you learn intuitively from such a teacher.

If you wish to take singing exams, the teacher should know the standards that are required at various levels and should be able to advise you on suitable exams and to prepare you for them. The same is true of recitals, competitions and auditions. If you are taking lessons privately (that is, outside of a school or conservatory environment), the singing teacher may be your point of contact with the world of amateur, academic and professional music-making and with performance opportunities.

On the technical level, it is obviously useful for the teacher to be able to identify quickly both individual strengths and areas that need work, and to take appropriate action. Here again, experience is a useful tool. On the other hand, taking lessons from a teacher who is herself an advanced singing student has advantages. This kind of teacher will have access to her own teacher and to other professionals at her own and higher levels, so that she has a network of contacts with whom she discusses singing technique. She lives, breathes and sings 'singing'.

Regardless of the degree of formality in the relationship, the teacher should maintain a positive, professional attitude towards her students and take a keen interest in seeing them learn and approach their potential. She creates an atmosphere of mutual respect and good humour in the studio which the student learns to associate with the practice and performance of music. Experience has given her both insight into her students' potential and an instinct for how to develop it. She demands the highest standards of commitment and behaviour from her students and from herself.

A singing teacher who values herself generally has no time for students who lack the commitment necessary to achieve their potential. Consistent lateness or lack of musical preparation, insufficient or desultory practice, false enthusiasm and constant excuses on the part of the student are rarely tolerated. She has had experience with students who come to every lesson with their practice conscientiously done, music thoughtfully prepared, questions about technique and about the music bubbling out of them, interested and eager to get on with the lesson. The good teacher is an expert at spotting lack of commitment and integrity in the unrealistic or uninterested student or the student who believes that she is such a star that she doesn't need to do any work.

On the other hand, she must also realise that, for most students, music is not their whole life, and they have other needs and commitments as well. She should not make the student feel that nothing is ever good enough. The ground rules for mutual expectations should be made clear during the first meeting. If the student is planning a professional career and the teacher is taking her on with that goal in mind, she has a right to expect that the student will make certain sacrifices in order to achieve her goal. Indeed, the student needs to be aware of this herself. If the student is just singing for fun, then the teacher needs to know this, too, and should suggest some guidelines for productive practice that will fit into her schedule.

On your part, do not assume that a teacher's time outside the lesson is at your disposal, and that you can ring her at any time for a chat or to ask questions, or that the teacher should give you extra time in your lesson if you want it. Singing teachers vary in the amount of freedom that they allow in this.

The teacher is expected to have a good working knowledge of interpretation, performance practice in various periods of music, languages, suitable repertoire, musical considerations. Some of these areas are the province of specialists, so she may have only a general knowledge, but she should be able to point the student in the direction of finding out some of the answers for herself. Some singing teachers are pianists. The primary purpose, whether she is a fine pianist or not, is for her to teach vocal technique. She should be able to provide guidance on contemporary performance styles and practice.

Singing teacher, voice coach, accompanist – what's the difference?

A singing teacher works on vocal technique; she teaches the student how to sing.

While a voice coach may reinforce singing technique, her main role is to teach certain aspects of the music. This includes an often profound and extensive knowledge of languages and their pronunciation, historical and contemporary performance practice, operas, their literary origins and performance history, interpretation of art song and their historical and musical context and acoustic considerations.

A répétiteur is also a voice coach, but usually specialises in operatic roles, and is often associated with a particular opera company.

The voice coach is usually an accompanist, too. An accompanist, is, however, not always a voice coach; she may accompany other instrumentalists as well as singers or play in other ensembles, and may lack certain skills specific to the voice coach. A fine accompanist, whether or not she is also a voice coach, is an invaluable ally during a performance of any kind: audition, recital, exam or whatever. She will subtly reinforce all that is best in the singing, and will inconspicuously get the singer through the rough bits.

At the most basic level, the accompanist will 'bash out' notes for the singer if she simply cannot learn the music any other way. Unless this was part of the agreement from the outset, this should be avoided, since most accompanists will rightly feel that their time is being wasted. The responsibility to learn the notes belongs to the singer.

The language coach specialises in teaching pronunciation for singers. Often a native speaker, she may be able to provide insight into the interpretation of the poetry as well, but this is not her main purpose.

Auditioning for a singing teacher

A singing teacher will want to hear a prospective student before she makes a commitment. She will want to know what the student's goals are and whether she can help the student achieve them. She will also be looking for indications that she and the student will be able to work together productively.

She will probably run through a few exercises and make a few suggestions. This serves several purposes: she can evaluate the voice; she can see how quickly the student picks up both musical and verbal ideas; she also puts the student at ease – yes, remarkably, while the student is being tested, the mere act of singing will put her at ease. The teacher will ask to hear some music. For a beginner, this can be a very simple piece – a folk song, a pop song, anything that has been prepared and that shows that voice at its best. The teacher is looking not only for the voice, but also for a certain level of preparation and a certain commitment to the music that are far more important than the voice. While the singer is looking for a good teacher, the teacher is looking for a good student. This is true at any level.

On a more advanced level, the teacher may ask the prospective student what she has done professionally, and whether she has an agent. The student at this level will probably already have submitted a CV to the teacher. She may have to, or want to, bring her own accompanist to the audition lesson.

Hard facts

The fact is that there is no 'magic wand' school of training. As with any skill, the singer must be prepared to put in the time that it takes to learn the instrument (the voice) and the material (the musical skills). Singing teachers are often asked how long it takes to learn to sing. The quick answer is 'between five and eight years'. The more complex and truthful answer is that the singer never stops learning about the voice and about how to sing.

The fact that singing is a complex skill – like speaking, skiing or riding a horse – means that it takes a certain length of time to incorporate the intellectual grasp of singing (at both the conceptual and the conscious level) into a complete set of fine, automatic physiological responses that are characteristic of the finished singer.

Alternatives

Voice training is a time-consuming and expensive undertaking, and, if the singer is interested in a professional career, there is no shortcut. Certain resources, however, that are available to everyone, can be very useful in learning how to sing.

Listening

The student learns through close, attentive and focused listening to the kind of singing and singers that she aspires to. This is, in fact, how people who 'sing naturally' have learnt to sing. They have almost always been surrounded, from an early age, by people who sing well. Children pick up the sound automatically. Adults can do exactly the same, but they have to focus on it as openly and naively as children. They have to be willing to listen uncritically, in a purely childlike and curious way, by disengaging their brains temporarily. Adults can then return in memory to what they have heard and choose to listen again, this time analytically, bringing the force of their prior knowledge and experience into the process.

Mimicking

Children are usually rebuked for rudeness when they mimic others and by the time they reach adolescence, they have lost or repressed the skill. Yet so much of our aural learning originates in our ability to mimic sounds. Mimicking the sounds of a favourite singer is one of the best ways of learning how she sings. And it is a more natural, or at least a more childlike, way of learning than the intellectual process described in this book. Mimicry bypasses the intellectual step. Both are useful paths to the same goal. One school of thought embraces the idea that all singing is mimicry of an ideal voice.

Singing

Singing is the goal, the tool and the process. To sing everywhere and under all circumstances, to sing in ensembles and with the rest of the family while doing chores, is to learn how to sing.

Chapter 7:

Singing Solo in Public

Training the voice can help anyone improve her voice and increase her enjoyment of singing. For many singers, however, the whole point of learning to sing is to increase their chances of obtaining opportunities to sing in public. Before the telephone starts to ring with offers, however, it is up to the singer to do her groundwork. This may mean examinations or auditions for musical organisations, conductors or agents. It may mean participating in singing competitions and music festivals at a local, national or international level. Gaining experience and making contacts in these ways can lead to offers of performing opportunities at many levels in recitals, oratorio, opera, musical theatre or church solo singing. Whether you are singing for a panel of judges in a formal examination, or giving a recital for the local university concert series, you are singing solo in public. This chapter is designed to be used by any singer at any stage of proficiency who wishes to perform in public. The novice singer will find more than she actually needs, and the professional may want to seek additional information.

Singing for an audience challenges your nerves while it rewards your hard work. For many singers, the 'buzz' of performing before people is the thing that makes all those hours of practice and preparation worthwhile! If you are one of those who enjoys the technical challenge of learning how to sing, you may find that public performance gives an edge to your technical skill that you didn't know you possessed. In any case, if you want to perform as a soloist, you'll soon be facing the challenge of singing in public or for a panel of judges. If your ambition is to sing in a community or church choir, you may still be called upon to audition with a solo piece. This chapter will provide you with information and skills that will help you face the challenges of solo singing in public.

Few of us enjoy being judged, but singing for a panel of judges gives us valuable opportunities to try out skills and get an informed opinion of our progress. The wealth of music festivals, competitions, examinations and auditions that are open to the singer are chances to gain this feedback. Each of these has a different purpose. Music festivals on a local or national scale are popular in the UK and in Canada, although they are less so in the United States. Music festivals often contain a wide variety of categories that run the gamut from tots lisping out nursery rhymes, to semi-professional young singers presenting operatic arias or short recital programmes. Winners of the top categories in festivals may go on to participate in more rigorous competitions, and to have international careers, while entrants in the festival's lower categories get a taste of the system and the opportunity to rub shoulders with the more experienced. Competitions at every level abound in North America and Europe, from school level where the prize is a certificate of merit, to televised competitions in which young professionals compete for thousands of pounds, recording contracts and international prestige.

Competing at a level that is comfortable for you can provide several benefits, even if you don't win. You can expect to be given comments by a judge (or panel of judges) who is competent and knowledgeable. At the school level, this may be the head of the music department at a neighbouring high school. At the top levels, the panel may comprise half a dozen singers, directors and conductors of international repute. To be a semi-finalist or finalist in such a competition carries a great deal of prestige in itself, and even those who do not win the top prize attract a great deal of attention.

Exams are designed to evaluate your level of competence. Examination boards in Britain and Canada require that you sing music from certain lists, which is carefully selected to challenge certain vocal skills. You are given a mark and a certificate, and the judge(s) normally give comments which aim to be helpful and constructive. Auditions, festivals, competitions and exams – in this section we'll call them 'performances' for the sake of simplicity – all have two things in common: first, you are being judged as a singer; second, you prepare for any of them in more or less the same way.

Masterclasses are a hybrid form. They are neither public performances – in the strictest sense of the word – nor are they judged. A masterclass is a 'one-off' meeting of a group of singers with a professional singer, singing teacher or vocal coach. In some respects, it is like a singing lesson held in public. Each of the singers presents a prepared piece of music to the rest of the group, and the teacher works with that singer on the music. The other singers observe, listening to the teacher's advice and its effect on the singer's performance. There is usually an opportunity for discussion. Then the next person will sing, and so on. Singers have the challenge of singing for their peers and the opportunity to learn from someone who is often a well-known singer or accompanist.

At their best, masterclasses provide a non-judgmental and healthy atmosphere in which singers learn from each other's efforts. Sometimes these masterclasses last a couple of hours, while others are held over a period of one or two days, and they may be open to the public. Even if you are not ready to participate as a singer, it is well worth attending these if you can, since you will undoubtedly gain an insight into various aspects of musical training, vocal technique and performing. Many music schools and universities hold masterclasses from time to time, which may be open to the public.

In addition to presentations of music which are judged or used as teaching experiences, the other category of vocal presentation is, of course, the performance itself. If you are singing in an ensemble such as an opera company, musical theatre group or band, the decisions about practice, rehearsals, costumes, publicity and schedules will be out of your hands. If you are organising a solo recital at a local venue, these responsibilities may fall on your own shoulders.

Preparation for a solo performance

Whether you are preparing for an audition, an exam or a competition, or for a recital or other solo public performance, much of the preparation is the same. An approach to general musical preparation has been suggested in Chapter 5, *Musical Skills*, but in this chapter the emphasis is on practical and mental preparation for public performance. In fact, the cardinal rule is *Be prepared in every way*. This means addressing each of the steps in the following 'Countdown to professional success', forgetting none of the points, and leaving nothing to chance. This outline can be used as a checklist from the time you decide to enter a competition, obtain a recital date or an audition, or apply to do an examination. Each point is explained more fully in the section that follows the outline.

Your preparation is the hallmark of your commitment to your performance. At any stage and at any level of performance or competition, and indeed in singing lessons, there is nothing easier for the audience, panel of judges or teacher to spot than an open lack of commitment, or the pretence of commitment which indicates, at best, naivety, and at worst, lack of integrity. Listeners will forgive many of the technical shortcomings that are easily exposed in performance, but they will not readily forgive, and will probably never forget, a singer's lack of commitment.

Countdown to professional success

First things first, plus ongoing habits:

1. Fill in any necessary forms and get them in on time.

2. Find out what music will be required.

3. Find out the date, time and place of the performance. (Here, as elsewhere in this section, 'performance' includes auditions, examinations, etc. – any presentation of solo singing in public.)

4. Buy originals of the music for yourself and your accompanist.

5. Learn the music.

6. Arrange for specialist coaching.

7. Practise often with your accompanist.

8. Make arrangements to rehearse with the performance accompanist, if necessary/possible.

9. Practise your music six days a week.

10. Visualise success.

11. If the performance is in a foreign country, give yourself time to organise transportation and accommodation. Your passport should always be up to date.

Four weeks before:

12. Arrange for haircut, manicure ...

13. Practise with the accompanist you will have for the performance, if possible.

14. Make sure you have suitable publicity photographs.

15. Double check all the details.

16. Prepare suitable clothing.

17. Arrange transportation to and from the venue. Arrange hotel accommodation if necessary.

18. Update your CV if necessary.

19. Have a run-through of the recital.

The day before:

20. Check clothing (and make-up).

21. Mark your music, and that of your accompanist, if you

have it, with Post-it notes. Gather together your CV, photos, and any other paperwork that is required.

On the day:

22.   Be early.

23.   If you haven't met the accompanist before ...

24.   Be professional in both attitude and behaviour.

25.   When it's all over, enjoy the experience!

The countdown in detail

INITIAL STAGES:

1.   Fill in the forms and get them in on time.

Be meticulous. Take a photocopy, or retain the completed application as a computer file, if appropriate.

Keep your musical CV and publicity photographs up to date so that you won't have to think about them each time you need them. Even so, each time you send out a CV, it should be customised to answer the needs of the person or institution to whom you're sending it. The CV should be printed on good quality paper and look thoroughly professional. Use the spellcheck program on your computer. If you're unsure of the spellings of professional institutions, accompanists you have worked with, places you have performed – check them out and get them right. Your CV and photographs represent you in your absence. You don't want them to say that you are careless.

Your CV should include the following:

Name under which you perform.

Date of birth.

Current address.

Home telephone number. If you include your mobile number, make sure to keep it up to date.

Email address.

Web address, if you have one.

Agent, if you have one. Include contact details.

Qualifications. Include voice qualifications first (e.g. Standard grade music, ARCM, etc.). Include marks of distinction or merit. Include masterclasses. If you are struggling to find things here, call the category 'Study and Qualifications', and include related study you have undertaken, even informally, such as drama classes, theatre workshops, piano lessons, etc.

Prizes, if applicable. In reverse chronological order. Include festivals, competitions, etc.

Voice category. Even if you are auditioning for a specific role, keep this category fairly generalised. For example, you may believe yourself to be a lyric coloratura soprano, and you send your CV to a semi-professional company asking for an audition for the role of Gilda in *Rigoletto*. The auditioning committee may, however, be looking for a lyric soprano for the role. In the event, the voice-type that they have in mind may correspond to your idea of a lyric coloratura, but there is no point in creating an unnecessary misunderstanding. Similarly, if you are auditioning for a repertory opera company, you will want to make yourself seem as versatile as possible.

Singing teachers. List chronologically, the most recent first.

Operatic roles (or solo roles in musical theatre). List in reverse chronological order, including the company, venue, year of performance. Distinguish between school performances and professional engagements.

Oratorio. As above.

Recitals (or solo performances as singer in a band, etc.). As above.

Other performing experience. As above. This might include CDs, theatre, radio or television appearances, performances on another instrument, videos, film, etc. If you have limited experience as a soloist, but have sung in a chorus, include this here.

Future engagements. If you really have none, omit this category, but if you can devise something, it will look better. Here, as everywhere, be truthful, but don't sell yourself short either.

Referees. This is not always necessary. Be sure you ask your potential referees first to see whether they are willing to be contacted.

You should also have available up-to-date publicity photographs and biographical details suitable for inclusion in programme notes. Since these photos must follow certain size and format requirements, they should be taken by a professional photographer who is experienced in taking this type of picture. All you need is a head shot, but the style of the photo can range from the simple to the dramatic. The best will try to show the character of the singer as well as indicate the character of her voice. An effective photo of a soprano who sings the soubrette repertoire might emphasise the quality of lightness and mischievousness of many of her roles. The photo of a spinto soprano could well be more dramatic, utilising contrasts of light and darkness to emphasise the deeper, more sombre undercurrents of the characters she portrays. An experienced photographer should know how to create these effects on your behalf.

Biographical details should be kept up to date. These are useful for programme notes or newspaper publicity. They contain some of the same information that appears in the CV, but paragraph format is used. The style is informal, almost chatty, but compressed. Audiences are interested in you as a performer and as a person, so a certain amount of personal autobiographical detail is welcome here.

Keep a folder with originals and copies of reviews. It's better to keep these in a folder than in a scrapbook, since you'll want to photocopy them. You're keeping them for practical, not sentimental, reasons. If you have been reviewed in major newspapers or journals, you may be able to download reviews from online sources and maintain a computer file of these, which can be printed out as necessary.

Having a CD of your singing can also be useful. If you make one for general purposes, it should contain a wide enough repertoire to show what you can do. However, in many cases, you will be asked to sing specific music, and it is hard to second guess what you'll need.

2.   Find out exactly what music will be required.

You may be expected to prepare a particular piece or pieces. You may be given a choice from a limited list, or you may be allowed to sing a piece or pieces of your own choice. If the choice is yours, you must make sure to find out how many pieces you'll need. Also find out what kind of music to prepare; this seems elementary, but it is futile and unnecessary to come to an audition with a German Lied if an operatic aria is required, or with two arias in English if one is supposed to be in a foreign language. The same is true of examinations. Make sure you know precisely how many pieces you'll need to sing from each list, and that the syllabus you are using is current.

If you can sing music of your own choice in an audition or competition, choose pieces that show off your voice at its best. The people who are auditioning you want to hear something special. If you have an unusually large range or great vocal flexibility, show them these qualities. This doesn't necessarily mean that you need to sing a long piece. An experienced panel will be quick to spot your ability. Choose something from the standard repertoire; there is no reason to assume that the accompanist will be familiar with a little-known piece, and she will be better able to support your singing if she is not sight-reading the piano part.

If several pieces are required, choose music that shows contrasting mood, tempo and key. The panel of judges may start to squirm if they have to sit through three pieces all of which are marked *allegretto* and are in the key of E with a ¾ time signature.

3.   Find out the date, time and place of the performance.

If you are unfamiliar with the venue, get directions. Put the information in your diary, along with phone numbers and email addresses of contacts in case of slip-ups. Find out whether you will be expected to provide your own accompanist or to use one provided for you. If the latter, find out whether you will be able to rehearse with her beforehand. Make arrangements to practise with her, if it is feasible. If it is too early for this, find out when you should do this. If you want to use a CD accompaniment, check to see whether this is allowed or expected, and make sure that the accompaniment is in the right key.

If you are giving a recital in a hall, find out precisely what you are responsible for. At some point, you will want to check out the hall and, if you can, rehearse in it. Check the action and the condition of the piano. Find out if it will be tuned for your performance. Introduce yourself to the backstage crew and familiarise yourself with the lighting arrangements and the curtain protocol. Check the lighting in relation to the position of the piano. Have someone with a good critical eye check you out from the hall. Your bone structure, especially eyes and cheekbones, can look haggard with the wrong lighting. Moving six inches upstage may make the difference between basking in the limelight or hiding in the shadows. If the hall is a popular or famous venue, you will be competing for time in it with many other performers, so it is unwise to assume that you will be able to make arrangements whenever you wish.

4.   Buy originals of the music for yourself and, if necessary, for your accompanist.

Never use photocopies in performance. It is illegal under most circumstances. Make sure that the music is in the correct key and in the right format – if you are singing a song from a show, for example, use the piano/vocal version, not an SATB version or any other. Above all, make sure that your edition and that of the accompanist are the same. Different editions may contain markings, repeats, musical notes and even melodies that are at variance with one another. It is unrealistic to expect yourself or your accompanist to remember these on the day.

Ensure that the music you give to your accompanist for the performance is in good condition. Loose pages have a habit of falling out and flying offstage during performances. Lighting conditions in halls are not always ideal, so the music must be legible and not dog-eared. If the accompanist is going to be using a full score or other large book, try to make sure that the book will stay open on the piano. If the song is one of many in a book, mark the page with a Post-it note. Pages should be easy to turn, especially if there is no page-turner and the accompanist has to turn them herself. You, of course, will be singing from memory.

5.   Learn the music.

This is covered in Chapter 5. If you are preparing for an examination in singing, you can find out the expected criteria for that grade – know what they are, and make sure that you demonstrate these standards in your singing.

6.   Specialist coaching. Arrange for specialist coaching if necessary with voice teachers, vocal coaches, language coaches and acting coaches. See Chapter 6.

7.   Practise as often as you can with your accompanist.

8.   If it is possible to practise with the accompanist you will have for the performance, make arrangements to do so as early as possible. Her time is limited and others will want to book as well.

9.   Practise six days a week.

One of the easiest things to do at this stage is to put things off. Arrange to put on performances for friends and family before the actual event.

10. Mental preparation.

The visualisation techniques given in Chapter 2 are useful throughout your preparation. It is particularly helpful to 'sing' through parts of the programme silently, but in real time, each night before going to bed, when you are in a relaxed frame of mind.

11. If the performance is in a foreign country, give yourself time to organise transportation and accommodation.

Your passport should always be up to date. Foreign travel arrangements should be made as early as possible.

FOUR WEEKS BEFORE:

12. Arrange for haircuts, manicures and professional make-up.

Your hair should be appropriate to the type of music you sing. Whatever the style, your face should be visible, not covered or overpowered by your hair. Start thinking about suitable clothing.

13. Practise with the accompanist you will have for the performance.

Establishing a sound working relationship with this accompanist will reap rewards in the short term, when you do your audition (or other performance). In the long term, working with different accompanists is very useful. If the accompanist is a seasoned professional, she will have an insight into the interpretation, phrasing, tempo and other aspects of the music.

14. Make sure that you have enough publicity photographs.

15. Double-check everything.

16. Prepare suitable clothing.

Pop and rock singers generally get it right, since their music is part of an entire culture. Singers of classical music, unfortunately, are not always as conscious of how they present themselves. Clothing should always be smart, flattering, up to date, and of the best quality you can afford. The colour is important, too. On the recital stage, pastels are often washed out by brilliant lighting, and white or cream can look characterless. Black may be chic, but you'll look very gloomy if you are entirely covered in it. If you decide on black, add another colour close to the face, or expose arms and shoulders. Warm and bright colours work well onstage. This goes for make-up, too. Modern performance practice is for an elegant and understated look, but that doesn't mean casual. If possible, arrange to have your recital make-up done by a professional with experience in this sort of work. Above all, your clothing for any performance should be comfortable, and you should feel at home in it. There's no point in trying to sing in a gorgeous designer suit that's too tight in the waist, or a skirt in which you feel self-conscious about chubby knees. Make sure you have an extra pair of tights in the right colour. Don't wear clothing that is out of date. The stage magnifies both flaws and features. Don't wear clothing or accessories that will distract the panel or get in your way while you are on stage or walking across the stage or up steps. Slingback or backless shoes clump noisily up steps that lead to the stage; bangle bracelets rattle each time you move your arm; dangling earrings catch the stage lights and flash annoyingly into the eyes of the audience.

Performance clothing for men should be comfortable, contemporary and very smart. That ten-year-old suit that you've had since your student days will not do. The stage emphasises shabbiness and lack of care.

17. Arrange transportation to and from the venue. Book hotels, if necessary.

18. Make sure that your CV is up to date.

19. Have a run-through of the performance with your accompanist, make-up, clothing, page-turner, everything as it will be on the day of the performance.

Don't forget to invite an audience of friends. If you are giving a recital, it would be wise to have this run-through at the concert venue.

THE DAY BEFORE:

20. Check clothing and make-up.

21. Make sure your music is organised and ready to go.

Mark the pages of scores or anthologies with Post-it notes. Have a waterproof wallet or envelope for music and other papers. Include publicity photos and extra copies of your CV.

ON THE DAY:

22. Never, never fail to show up for an audition, recital, competition or any other type of performance.

It will be remembered and it will count against you. From the time you send in your application forms, your professional behaviour is on display. Your behaviour on the day is only the final stage. If you absolutely must cancel – which you would do only under the most serious circumstances – you must get a message to the panel beforehand. Follow up later with an apology and an explanation. The most important rule for the solo performer is this: there are no excuses.

When you get to the audition hall, or the exam venue, be prepared for anything. You may arrive a judicious twenty minutes early only to find that you will have to wait forty minutes in a freezing corridor, but never assume that auditions run late. As often as not, they run on time or even early. Rushing to the hall at the last minute will not contribute to your sense of security, nor will it endear you to the panel if they have been waiting for you. There will usually be someone at the entrance to the hall who is organising the entrants. If there is no one there, wait. Never go into the hall while someone is singing on stage. Take a few moments to settle your nerves, breathe deeply and relax. It may be possible to warm up in another room. The situation, and the atmosphere, will be a little different in each case. Give yourself time to settle down for a few minutes and get your bearings.

23. If your accompanist is provided for you and you have not had the opportunity to rehearse with her, it's possible that you may have a few minutes to discuss tempi and cuts with her. You can't count on this, however.

24. Be professional.

When you are invited to go into the hall, you must get your bearings quickly, taking in the set-up of the stage, the steps leading to it and the whereabouts of the panel of judges. The judges will have your paperwork before them, and they may ask you for extra copies of your CV or other information. If you are nervous, you may tend to rush. If so, slow yourself down to an unhurried but purposeful pace in walking, speech and movement. If you have your own accompanist with you, lead the way to the stage. If the accompanist is already on the stage and you have not rehearsed with her or discussed the music with her, give her the music in the order you think you will be singing it.

When you're in place, one of the panel members will normally invite you to begin with a nod or by saying, 'What would you like to sing?' You may take a very brief moment to show the accompanist any cuts in the music, if you have not had the opportunity to do so earlier. Even if the piece has been set and you have no choice in the matter, you may announce your piece with the name of the aria and the opera, or the song and the composer. Don't give them too much information. They know the piece; it is you they're interested in. Speak up clearly without mumbling or shouting.

If you are given a choice, sing your 'best piece' first. You can't count on being asked to sing another, so there's no point in saving the best for last. You may have been asked to prepare several pieces, but there's no guarantee you'll be asked to sing them all.

The panel will be judging you on several points: presentation, diction and communication in a foreign language, intelligibility, intonation, voice quality and suitability for their needs (if applicable), musicality and musicianship, vocal technique, interpretation and stage presence.

Many singers wonder how much acting they should do on stage. Whether you are singing in a competition, an exam, a recital or an audition, the answer is the same: unless you are singing in a staged performance, any acting that you do on stage should be done with the voice and the eyes. Grimacing or throwing the arms about will not help to express classical music. Having stated this general rule, it is necessary to add that many people break it, and do so charmingly. If you are at all in doubt about your ability to carry it off, it is better to err on the side of caution. When you attend recitals and other public performances, pay close attention to this aspect of singers' stage manner.

If you are a pop or rock singer auditioning for an agent, your singing may be part of a routine that includes stylised movement and dance. If this is the case, then by all means do your act. Classical singers would do well to choreograph their performances with the same attention to detail.

Subtle eye contact can make or break a performance, but it is not always appropriate. An aria is part of a dramatic work, not a direct communication with the audience; the general rule is not to make eye contact with the audience. Concert arias (such as those by Mozart or Rossini, for example), oratorio arias and certain songs which seem to be part of a larger narrative, can also be treated this way, but it depends upon the text. Performances of folk song and art song, by contrast, benefit from the use of eye contact. The phrase 'keep the eyes soft', used in the practice of yoga and other Eastern arts, is useful. The singer who stares fixedly at the lady in the back row with the back-combed hair is going to make everyone uncomfortable, while the singer whose gaze is constantly jumping up and down and back and forth is giving a visible display of her own lack of focus. It is probably insensitive to catch and hold the eye of an elderly member of the auditioning committee in order to sing to him, 'Er ist tot' ('He is dead'). Eye contact with the audience may be impossible during recitals, when the auditorium is dark.

Your stage presence is part of your performance, and your professional and personal behaviour is on display at all times. Do not be put off by anything that may occur while you are singing. People may wander in and out of the room, tube trains may rumble by, outside in the alley a pack of feral dogs may be rifling the dustbins under the open window, but, unless you are asked by the panel to stop, take no notice and keep singing.

You will be judged not only on how you communicate the music, but how you treat the panel and the accompanist. As part of the judges' evaluation of your audition, they may engage you in a discussion about your performance or your career. They may ask for another piece. If they do, sing one that contrasts with the first. Don't despair if you're not asked for another. They may have decided already that they want you, but they're running late and they still have four singers to hear before they can break for coffee. If they listen to only one piece and merely say, 'Thank you', smile and thank them. Turn with a smile to thank the accompanist, take your music and leave the stage quickly and graciously.

Do not be put out if they have listened to only one piece. More than one singer, thinking that she has failed to make the grade, has scowled unthinkingly at the panel, only to discover later that it was the scowl that cost her the role. Always behave generously and graciously towards other musicians, on and off stage, no matter how trying the circumstances. This may seem like gratuitous advice, but disappointment and hurt feelings often show on our faces as jealousy or resentment, and will be interpreted as such. Like the face in your publicity photograph, the face you present on stage will be identified with you. The other competitors deserve to be treated with respect, too, regardless of their performance.

25. When it is all over, enjoy the positive energy that flows from the experience.

Reward yourself and save the rehashing until later; then deal with it in a calm, uncritical manner. Talk it through with other singers who have been through the process and with your teacher. What can be improved? What have you learnt about yourself and your singing under stressful conditions? What surprised you about your performance? What do you need to work on? What do you do best? There will be aspects of the experience that you particularly enjoyed. What were they? How can you bring the enjoyment to the other parts of the process? Analysing the performance in this way can be made into a constructive learning process.

A word on auditioning for local or community groups

Many people find the thought of joining a choir or other singing group for the first time rather daunting. Perhaps you know someone who sings in the choir who can offer reassurance. If not, most choirs have a membership secretary. This is usually someone who is outgoing and enthusiastic about the choir. She'll be happy to talk to you about any aspects of membership that may be worrying you. It could be that some knowledge of the procedures and the standards that are expected will be enough to calm your fears.

Amateur choirs tend to be very friendly groups. They're often actively looking for singers and you may find yourself being recruited without an audition. Some, of course, do require an audition, but making contact with a friendly face or a friendly voice on the telephone can go a long way to reassuring you. Take the first step.

The recital

The recital is similar in many aspects to the exam and the audition. The difference is that this solo performance is for an audience rather than a committee of judges and you enjoy a greater amount of freedom in determining your programme. You will, however, be responsible for many things that you have no control over in the other instances – the state and tuning of the piano, the lighting of the hall, the flowers, publicity.

Entire books have been written on the subject of recital planning and presentation. Attend as many recitals as you can, notice what works and what doesn't and by all means read as much of the current literature on the subject as you can. Read what the critics have to say about recitals in both local and national newspapers. The hallmark of the recital is variety. In practice, this can mean a programme in which the theme of 'spring' includes music by Mozart, Schubert, Richard Strauss and Fauré. Or it can mean an entire programme of nineteenth- and twentieth-century French music. Or it can mean an entire programme of music by Schubert, or of settings by different composers of the poetry of Goethe. Variety is achieved in a number of ways: tempo, key, language, rhythm, mood, poetry.

In the recital, you will have greater opportunity to let your general creativity flourish. The clothing of the singer and the accompanist can be coordinated in terms of style, degree of formality and colour. Consider your own attire when planning the size and colours of the flowers and other shrubbery on stage. If you are petite, you may be overwhelmed by potted palms, and if you are tall or strongly built, try to avoid fussy little arrangements in favour of one or two sizeable and dramatic ones. Don't forget the page-turner, if you have one. She is meant to be invisible, but the opposite will be true if she is wearing scruffy jeans while you and your accompanist are resplendent in evening gowns. It is not necessary for her to dress as formally as the performers, but some thought should be given to the style of her dress, too. (And, although she's meant to be invisible during the performance, she should be acknowledged with thanks backstage. It was due to her that the awkward page turn back to the beginning of the 'A' section was achieved so gracefully by your accompanist.)

You will probably want to be responsible for your own programme notes and translations. The programme is your calling card, and will represent you in the minds of the audience and critics after the performance is over. There are many styles of programme, from the very plain to the elaborate. The most important thing is to present clearly what you are going to perform, in the order you are going to perform it. The composers' names and dates are normally printed to the right of the work, in a separate column. Programme notes may include a performance history of the music, and the audience will understand the music better if it can be put into a historical or cultural context. Translations should be accurate in the literal sense: no one is expecting you to be a great poet, but the translations should also remain true to the spirit of the poem, an aspect which is often lost in a literal translation. If you do not know the language, have the poetry translated by someone who does. (You should do this anyway, so that you know what the text means.) The English translations of texts which appear beneath the original words in the score, or on a page preceding the music, are often poor and even meaningless.

You may have to share the Green Room before and after the performance. It is very easy to get overexcited and to talk too much, but save your voice. Don't rehash past experiences, especially negative ones. You'll be with other performers and soloists, some of whom come off stage complaining about the unresponsive audience, the conductor who takes a tempo different from the one he took in rehearsals, the cougher in the front row. Your job is to be so well prepared that nothing fazes you. Going over your music quietly and thoughtfully can help to settle you.

Judging whether or not to give an encore after a solo recital requires sensitive timing. If the audience seems to want more, you should have a minimum of two pieces to offer as encore pieces. These are generally short pieces that the audience is likely to recognise. It can be effective to offer a song that contrasts in character from the rest of the programme. If you have given a formal, difficult recital that relied heavily on Bach and Mozart and finished with a difficult contemporary piece, a show tune or an appropriate folk song can be very welcome. A concert that has consisted of mainly French and English music might end with an encore that is related to the programme in terms of language and period, but which contrasts with the final piece in mood, key and tempo. On the other hand, an eclectic programme that has already included a lot of variety may have as its encore a flashy aria. The encore is a gift to the audience in return for their attention and enthusiasm and it must be offered with warmth.

Singers sometimes talk from the stage to the audience. If the programme, translations and background information about the singer, the accompanist and the music have all been included in the programme leaflet, there is no reason to do so. Exceptions occur at the outset of the recital if there is a deviation from the programme, or at the end, to announce the name and composer of the encore.

Audiences come to recitals to enjoy themselves and to share a musical experience which has, for many, a profound emotional, spiritual and social meaning. They want you to do well, and they want you to enjoy yourself, too, although they may not realise this fact. If you have prepared yourself with energy, commitment and integrity, you can scarcely go wrong.

Chapter 8:

Frequently Asked Questions

---

1. Is it always necessary to learn foreign languages if you want to sing 'classical' music? Why don't we use translations?

If you want to sing art song (i.e. non-operatic classical music), then, yes, you should learn at least the basic pronunciation and grammatical structures of French, German and Italian. Operatic libretti are not generally considered to be of very high poetic quality, although there are many exceptions to this generalisation. However, when you are singing the art song of any country, you are singing the poetry of that country. Poetry is extremely difficult to translate without loss of meaning, rhythm and sound. Add to this the difficulty of setting syllables to musical notes, and the enormity of the task becomes evident.

For example, take the French phrase, 'je t'aime'. Most people would be able to translate this into the English, 'I love you'. You might think, however, that setting the English to music would cause some difficulty, since, on the face of it, the French phrase contains two syllables and the English phrase three. As it happens, there would be no problem here, since, when French poetry is spoken or sung, the inflected endings – in this case, the 'e' of 'aime' – are pronounced; so in both English and French, there are three syllables to be set to music.

Suppose, however, that you wanted to translate the German phrase, 'Ich liebe dich' into the English, 'I love you'. Here, the German has four syllables, the English, three. The music itself would have to be re-written to accommodate the translation. These are very simple examples. Often, exact connotations of words are virtually untranslatable.

Similarly, the sounds of poetry contribute much to its meaning, and composers of song are sensitive to the settings of the words in such a way as to emphasise meanings. For example, a song by Schumann or Schubert might contain the word 'rauschen'; in English, the word is 'to rustle'. The word is onomatopoeic in both German and English; that is, the sound of the word echoes the sense. The musical setting of this word might contain quiet, rapidly iterated semi-quavers (sixteenth notes) in the piano part, to convey the actual sound of rustling leaves. By contrast, the French word, 'se ratatiner', may be accompanied by a series of repeated staccato notes in the treble of the piano part to emphasise the effect of desiccation, a drying up of vital forces. To translate as 'to shrivel' or 'to dry up' and to sing these words to the same accompaniment is to lose the expressive poetic force of both the language and the setting.

These simple examples illustrate some of the problems in translation, and the need for the singer to learn at least something about the languages in which she sings. Even the deceptively easy songs that we often call 'folk' songs are inextricably bound up with the language in which they are written and passed down, and it is up to the singer to express their meaning in as sensitive a way as possible.

There are many courses offered in the common European languages, and the singer is encouraged to undertake at least a grounding in French, German and Italian. It is important to study the language with either a native speaker or with a teacher whose pronunciation is flawless, and to get a sense of the grammar as well. While vocabulary can be looked up in a good dictionary, making sense of the sentence structure of poetry is difficult in any language.

Finally, it is vital in all cases not to sing anything without a complete understanding of both the meaning of the words and of the entire poem. If the singer does not understand the poem, she cannot express the meaning of the song. Singing is all about expressing mood and conveying emotional impact. Not to understand the words of a song is to remove one of the most potent vehicles of its meaning.

A word about pronunciation. British and American singers whose native language is English are expected to be able to sing virtually without accent in German, French and Italian. British singers should, and American singers must, be able to sing in Spanish. Singers must be able to sing English with or without regional accents, depending on the origin of the music. An American, English or Scottish song, for example, should be sung with the pronunciation that is appropriate for the piece. It is important, however, not to take this so far that the pronunciation becomes mimicry.

2. My mouth gets very dry when I try to sing and no sound comes out. What can I do?

Stick out your tongue and bite it. The saliva will start to flow. If you have to do this on stage, keep the mouth closed while curling as much of the tongue as possible forward towards the lips and between the teeth; then bite down lightly. It works!

3. My throat feels tight when I sing. Is this correct? What should I be feeling in my throat?

Your throat should never feel tight or tense. Ordinarily, the only feeling that you should have in your throat is one of 'openness'. You should feel the space, not the muscles that are creating the space. Tension in the throat, whether or not it is visible, may be an indication of tension in the muscles surrounding the voice-box. Some singers mistakenly tighten this area in the belief that they are keeping the throat 'open'. In fact, the converse is true. If you are holding the muscles of the throat rigid, you must learn to relax this area.

For tension in the throat, do the following exercise. Read through the directions first, and then attempt the exercise. You are going to tense all the muscles of the face, head and throat. Starting with the face, tense all the muscles of the forehead, cheeks, nose and chin; tense the lips and tongue. Clench the teeth or hold them rigid. Tense the muscles of the neck; let the veins stick out. Really feel the tension everywhere in these areas, and hold the tension for several seconds. Then, on a slow, relaxed outward breath, release all the tension. Be aware of the relaxed feel of all the muscles. Now that you have read the instructions, do the exercise.

When you sing, there should be no more tension in your throat than there is at the moment you finish the exercise.

Many singers are not aware of tightness in the throat or jaw (see below), and claim to be perfectly relaxed even when the teacher and other listeners can hear the tension in the voice. This is a matter of self-awareness, since it is difficult to experience the tension *as* tension without ever having experienced a relaxation of the muscles.

4. What about tension in the jaw? I'm not aware of it when I sing, but my teacher says that I'm holding my jaw in a fixed, or rigid, position.

Tension in the jaw, like tension in the throat, interferes with the free and open production of the sound which is the ideal in healthy singing. The exercise designed to help correct tightness in the throat will also help you to gain relaxation of the jaw.

It is easier to correct tension in the jaw, since you can see it readily if you look into the mirror. You can also feel the tension if you lightly place the thumb of one hand beneath the chin and the first two fingers of the same hand on the chin between the bone and the lower lip. Sing 'ah' on a single tone; you should be able to move the chin freely up and down with the hand. If you cannot do so, do the tightening/relaxing facial exercise (in No. 3, above) several times each day to practise feeling the sensation of the loose jaw. Then, with your fingers holding the newly relaxed jaw as described above, sing (a few notes, part of an easy song, anything). The goal of this exercise is to learn the feeling of the relaxed jaw. Only constant self-awareness will break the habit of the tight jaw.

Don't over-do the exercise by repeating it over and over again. This is unnecessarily tiring. Awareness and vigilance, not mindless repetition, will correct the problem.

Singing scales on 'yah, yah, yah', etc., can help to free the jaw. Allow the 'yah' to move the jaw up and down in an exaggerated manner.

5. I've just started to sing in a choir, and I find it very disturbing not to be able to hear myself. How can I develop enough power to make myself heard?

When a group of people are singing the same note, the individuals in the group do not hear their own voices. In broad terms, hearing is one of the senses, and sound is the feedback (the thing you are aware of) from that sense, just as the sight of the thing you are looking at is the feedback from seeing. When you are singing, the sound of your own voice and the sounds of the other voices blend to create the feedback that you are hearing. Your own sound is going out, along with the sounds that the other individuals are making. You may be able to hear the person behind you, or the person beside you, to some extent, but this is a matter of direction.

It can be disconcerting for the singer who is not used to choral singing to feel her sound immersed and seemingly lost within the sound of the group. Children who begin singing in a children's chorus, or youngsters who enjoy singing with a parent or teacher from a very early age, generally do not experience this difficulty. They simply learn very quickly, and unconsciously, to adapt their 'hearing' to the sound made by the group. It can be harder for someone who is not used to this. The best remedy for this is simply to forget about it, if you possibly can, and listen to the sound of the group as a whole, as you try to blend with that sound. The important thing is to keep going. It's rather like keeping in step with the person you're walking with. If you want to match your pace to hers, you have to do it while you are walking. If you stop to figure out how to do it, you'll be left behind!

6. I've been told that I have trouble 'matching pitches'. Does this mean I'll never be able to sing?

Absolutely not! It can be learnt with the help of insight, practice and determination. The ability to 'match pitch' involves hearing a pitch from an external source, being able to internalise ('hear') that pitch in your own mind and then being able to re-produce it (sing it). With experience, the process of hearing (external), hearing (internal) and singing (reproducing) becomes virtually instantaneous. Almost anyone can learn to do it.

The process can fail at one or more of several points. You may be able to hear the pitch from the external source, but not hear it internally. This sounds contradictory, but some individuals can 'match pitch' when they hear it played on a piano, but not when it is sung to them. For others, the converse is true. In this case, it would be helpful to work with someone who is prepared to play (or sing) pitches with you and is able to guide you to the right pitch when you go wrong. It may also be useful to work with a tape that you make up for yourself, or with the help of another person. When you become more comfortable with single pitches, move on to patterns of pitches such as triads and five-note scales, as well as groups of random pitches.

Another individual may be able to hear the pitch internally but may be unable to reproduce it in her own voice. This is largely a matter of unfamiliarity with the singing voice. Singing in a choir, singing along with CDs, any type of singing, preferably undertaken along with the study of singing technique, will be useful here.

In either case, the solution will come with continued practice, rather than through analysis or intellectualisation.

7. I'd like to study singing with a teacher, but I don't want to lose the individuality of my own voice. Is there any way to learn how to sing better without sacrificing the uniqueness of the voice I've got?

It is an utter misconception that you will lose the individual character and sound of your own voice when you learn correct singing technique. The goal of vocal study is to enable the singer to find her own sound, not to obliterate it. The more knowledge you have about singing, the greater freedom you will gain to make the sound you wish.

This particular myth about singing stems, I believe, from a misunderstanding or partial knowledge about what it means to sing in a choir, when the voices become blended to create a single sound. It does not mean that every individual in the choir sounds like every other individual. It means that the individual voices work together to make a combined sound which is unique to the group. For example, Hattie, Flora, Hazel, Fiona and Claire are all trained singers who sing in a madrigal group. Each has a sound uniquely her own, but together their five voices blend to create a sixth sound which is characteristic of their group. If Flora goes on holiday and Jocasta, another experienced choral singer, substitutes for her, the group will have a subtly different sound from the one it had with Flora.

8. When I take a breath for singing, should I inhale through my mouth or my nose?

Inhaling through the nose will clean, warm and filter the air that you take in. From that point of view, it is a good practice. To inhale in this way, however, takes longer than to inhale through the mouth, and you will find that often the music will not allow you enough time to do so. Inhaling through the mouth has other advantages. It is easier to breathe deeply ('into the diaphragm') when you take the breath through the mouth. It also helps to open the throat into a position that is natural for singing. By all means breathe through the nose when you can, but only if the depth of your breath and the opening of your throat do not suffer as a result.

9. When I'm singing a song, I can't take a deep breath quickly enough. How can I get enough breath when there's not even a rest in the music?

It is not necessarily the amount of air that you take in that determines the quality and depth of the breath. What is important is to allow the breath to create depth in the abdomen in coordination with the expansion of the rib cage in front, sides and back. This means that when you first take in the breath to sing, the intake of air should create deep abdominal support. Each subsequent breath acts by reflex to maintain this depth. 'Holding on' with the abdominal muscles when you need to take a quick breath will merely cause tension, which will result in shallow breathing. By contrast, if you try to relax the muscles completely, you will not have enough time for the quick breath you need. Allow the natural, reflexive action of the muscles to do the work for you.

To feel this reflex action, take a good breath and sing 'nuh, nuh, nuh, nuh' on any note in the middle of your range, allowing a break in the sound between each syllable, but without deliberately taking a breath at those points. If you have started by correctly supporting the breath, you will feel a slight relaxation/contraction of the abdominals between each syllable. Now repeat the exercise, but allow the reflex action of the muscles to allow air to flow in at each 'relaxation' of the abdominals.

To equate the deep breath with 'a lot of breath' often leads, paradoxically, to very shallow breathing, when the shoulders lift and the upper part of the chest, shoulders and upper arms are thrown back. Breathing deeply means taking air deeply into the body while at the same time coordinating the action which establishes or re-establishes the support. It doesn't have to be a long, drawn-out breath.

10. I'd like to learn how to sing better, but I don't want to sound like an opera singer! Won't training my voice mean that I end up with a voice that I can't use for the kind of music that I want to sing?

No. Technically correct singing is healthy singing that gives you more, not fewer, choices. Musicians differentiate between technique and style. A trained violinist, for example, may choose to play a variety of styles from classical to jazz to blues, and the number of classical musicians who are choosing to 'cross over' into other styles of music has grown greatly in the past few years. Learning how to sing correctly will give you the freedom to sing without strain and without making constant adjustments that previously you may have found yourself making because of vocal limitations which stem from lack of technical control.

11. When I get nervous on stage, I run out of air. I can't get through the phrases and I end up having to breathe in the middle of words.

'Running out of air' is largely a misconception. You have either not taken the breath deeply enough, so that the breath you have is unusable, or you are not supporting the breath properly, so that the energy of the breath is being released without appropriate control.

There is no doubt that experience will help you to get over this aspect of nervousness. Frequent public performances will help you eventually to feel more comfortable, and you will be able to enjoy fully your own performance.

There are certain things you can do, however, to help you in the meantime. To avoid clavicular breathing which builds up unusable air in the upper chest and gets in the way of taking a proper breath that can be used to produce a singing tone, pay close attention to the depth, not the amount, of the breath you take in (see 10 above). Practise this in the studio or practice room until this method of breathing into the abdomen becomes habitual.

If you breathe deeply as described above, but you still 'run out of air', you are not supporting the breath. You may be allowing air to escape without actually using it to produce a singing tone.

Try to be aware of what is going on while you are performing. If you have thought through and practised the correct techniques for breathing and support, and they have become second nature to you in the practice studio, you should find that focusing on these processes during performance will not only help to improve your breath control, but may help to dissipate the nervousness as well! During the actual performance, try to be process-orientated: focus on your technique (that is, on your awareness and control of the process); think about what you're doing, not about your emotions. Try not to focus on the outcome, that is, 'I really want to do a good job', or, 'I'm so nervous I know I'm going to run out of air'. Eventually you'll get to the point where you can release both kinds of thoughts, and you'll simply enjoy the wonderful experience of sharing your music-making with an appreciative audience. It's worth it!

12. I'm spending a lot of money on singing lessons for my daughter, aged 16, but she doesn't practise regularly. She says that she doesn't need to, since she reads music well and can just go to her lessons and sing the music without preparation.

Singing lessons are about much more than simply singing through the music. She should be learning to train her muscles and her approach. She will get very little benefit from the lessons if she approaches them in this way.

13. My daughter, aged 15, nagged me for singing lessons but now finds it hard to discipline herself to practise regularly, even though she enjoys singing. Any suggestions?

Sometimes even an eager pupil can find it difficult to discipline herself to practise. A systematic regimen can begin to seem too much like work and too little like the enjoyable leisure pastime she has been used to. Reasoning with her might help, pointing out that she began voice lessons with particular goals in mind, and that goals soon begin to seem like failures if they are not pursued. It is often more helpful, however, just to do the following: ask her to agree that, upon coming home from school, she will set her music on the piano (or wherever she practises), open the music to the pages she needs to work on and open her workbook or lesson book to the most recent notes or suggestions made by her teacher. That's all she has to do. Sooner or later, the open music on the music stand will tempt her because it is ready and waiting for her. If the music still doesn't 'call' her, perhaps the voice lessons should be stopped until she begins to feel their absence.

14. I'm auditioning for a show and the songs sound better in my voice if I sing them using a starting pitch that is different from the ones in the musical score. Why can't I just transpose the piece and use whatever starting pitch I want?

There are many reasons. The accompanist who is playing for you will not necessarily be able to transpose at sight. If the performance is to be done with an orchestra, the orchestral parts are published in a particular key, all of which would have to be transposed. If for a show, your newly transposed part may not blend well with the parts of the other characters in the show. The auditioning committee is interested in finding a voice that suits the part as it is written.

15. How can I increase the range of my voice?

You increase the range of your voice by building the centre and learning how to approach the extremities. The vocal technique that is involved improves with practice, which will help to increase the range. Each voice is different, however, with a unique potential. The process cannot be rushed, since it involves re-educating certain muscles.

16. What should I eat before a performance?

This is a fraught question, with as many answers as there are singers. Experience is the best guide. Most singers avoid eating a heavy meal on the day of the performance. A light meal of fruit and toast, taken an hour or so before a performance, often provides the energy you need without leaving you feeling overly full. Others avoid carbohydrates completely, choosing a meal of salmon and lightly steamed vegetables. Some singers avoid dairy products, believing that they produce phlegm. Sugary foods produce a 'rush' of energy that soon dissipates and leaves a feeling of tiredness or lethargy. Sweet drinks increase thirst and, if the singer is prone to nerves, coffee can make the jitters even worse, so water is the best drink. Hot water with lemon and honey can be soothing to the throat and promote a feeling of well-being.

17. My throat hurts when I sing. Is this normal?

Absolutely not. If your throat hurts or feels sore or strained, do not sing. If the pain persists, see a doctor. If someone tells you that it is normal to feel pain or soreness while you're singing, or after you have sung, I'd advise you to walk away from that person as quickly as you can.

If you feel pain when you sing, you may have a physical problem, or you may be doing something wrong technically. In either case, persistent pain is not an option. Stop singing, find the source of the pain, and eliminate it.

You may feel that you are stretching the muscles of the pharynx. These muscles may retain the feeling of being stretched for an hour or two after you have stopped singing. This is all right, but do not place stress on the muscles by continuing to talk after you have sung. These muscles, like any other in your body, need a 'cool-down' phase. Don't over-tax them.

18. I've always sung in choruses, but now I'm taking singing lessons, and I find it hard to get through the phrases. When you're singing in a chorus, you can often mask a 'catch breath' in the middle of a word because you're covered by the rest of the section, and it is hard to get out of this habit. Any hints?

This is a habit that choral singers all too easily fall into, and you've passed the first hurdle if you are aware that you are carrying it into your solo singing as well. Mark the music – you should do this anyway – with phrasing and breath marks, so that you know precisely where you are going to breathe, and always read ahead to those points. The work that you do in your lessons and your own practice will help to increase the breath support that you need.

19. How can I project my voice so that it carries better?

There are no magical tricks that you can perform to project the voice. The better your breath support and placement (or focus), the better it will 'project'. These improve with knowledge and practice. The concept of placing the voice 'out in front' can be helpful. Choose a spot several inches or feet in front of you, or even at the back of the room, and think of placing the voice in that spot as you sing. Above all, avoid shouting or simply 'singing louder'.

20. I asked my choral conductor if I could take singing lessons from her, but she says she's not qualified. I assumed that she would know how to sing.

It is often thought that choral conductors are also voice teachers. While it may be true that a particular conductor is specifically qualified to teach singing, the fact that she is involved in directing voices does not make her a singing teacher. Teaching vocal technique and conducting choirs are both specialised subjects, requiring specialised training and knowledge. The choral conductor understands how to make the individual voices blend and how to get a particular sound and colour from the group that she has to work with, but she is not necessarily knowledgeable about the training of those voices on an individual basis. Her instrument is the choir.

Index

Books from Allworth Press

Allworth Press is an imprint of Allworth Communications, Inc. Selected titles are listed below.

The Quotable Musician: From Bach to Tupac
by Sheila E. Anderson (hardcover, 7½ × 7½, 224 pages, $19.95)

Making It in the Music Business: The Business and Legal Guide for Songwriters and Performers, Third Edition
by Lee Wilson (paperback, 6 × 9, 256 pages, $19.95)

Making and Marketing Music: The Musician's Guide to Financing, Distributing, and Promoting Albums, Second Edition
by Jodi Summers (paperback, 6 × 9, 240 pages, $19.95)

Creative Careers in Music, Second Edition
by Josquin des Pres and Mark Landsman (paperback, 6 × 9, 240 pages, $19.95)

Career Solutions for Creative People: How to Balance Artistic Goals with Career Security
by Dr. Ronda Ormont (paperback, 6 × 9, 320 pages, $19.95)

Gigging: A Practical Guide for Musicians
by Patricia Shih (paperback, 6 × 9, 256 pages, $19.95)

Rock Star 101: A Rock Star's Guide to Survival and Success in the Music Business
by Marc Ferrari (paperback, 5½ × 8½, 176 pages, $14.95)

The Songwriter's and Musician's Guide to Nashville, Third Edition
by Sherry Bond (paperback, 6 × 9, 256 pages, $19.95)